Dinosaurs of Power

Dinosaurs of Power

Matthew Petchinsky

Dinosaurs of Power: Unlocking Ancient Magick
By: Matthew Petchinsky

Introduction: Awakening the Power of Ancient Beasts

Dinosaurs, the colossal rulers of the prehistoric Earth, roamed our planet for over 165 million years, embodying an unparalleled essence of power, resilience, and adaptability. These ancient creatures were masters of their domain, thriving in diverse environments, adapting to shifting ecosystems, and leaving an indelible mark on Earth's history. Though they vanished from the physical plane millions of years ago, their essence and energy endure, embedded in the Earth's memory, fossils, and in the collective unconscious of humanity.

But what if this raw, untamed power didn't simply fade away? What if the energy of these majestic beings lingers in the mystical ether, waiting for us to tap into it? Just as we draw strength from the forces of nature, the cycles of the moon, or the alignment of the stars, so too can we harness the ancient magick of dinosaurs. They represent not just a biological marvel but a spiritual force—primordial archetypes of strength, adaptability, and dominance.

This book serves as a bridge between the prehistoric world and modern magickal practices, offering a path to connect with the profound energy of these ancient beasts. Whether you're seeking courage like the mighty Tyrannosaurus rex, patience and resilience like the Stegosaurus, or wisdom and balance like the Brachiosaurus, this guide will teach you how to channel these archetypes to enhance your magickal and personal journey.

The Power of Dinosaur Archetypes

Dinosaurs, in their sheer diversity, represent a wide range of energies and magickal archetypes. Each species embodies distinct qualities that we can incorporate into our lives and practices:

- **Tyrannosaurus rex** symbolizes ferocity, leadership, and unyielding confidence.
- **Brontosaurus** represents groundedness, stability, and quiet strength.
- **Pterodactyl** channels freedom, ascension, and a connection to higher planes.
- **Velociraptor** offers agility, strategy, and precision.
- **Ankylosaurus** serves as a protector and fortress against harm, shielding us from negativity.

By understanding the unique traits of these creatures, we can align ourselves with their energies, using them as guides in spellwork, meditation, and rituals. Each dinosaur becomes a spiritual ally, amplifying our intentions and offering a connection to the primordial essence of life on Earth.

Why Dinosaur Magick?

In modern magickal practices, we often turn to familiar sources of power: celestial bodies, natural elements, deities, and animal totems. However, the energy of dinosaurs is an untapped resource that predates all these systems. They were the original titans of Earth, embodying a connection to the planet that is primal and uncorrupted by modern influences.

Dinosaur magick is particularly potent for several reasons:

1. **Primal Energy:** Dinosaurs existed during an era of untamed natural forces. Their energy is raw, unfiltered, and immensely powerful, making it ideal for spells requiring strength, transformation, or protection.
2. **Ancestral Connection:** Fossils and the Earth itself retain the vibrational imprint of dinosaurs. Working with fossils or dinosaur symbols connects us to the ancient past and the wisdom of the Earth's memory.
3. **Universal Archetypes:** Dinosaurs resonate with universal themes like survival, dominance, adaptability, and extinction, offering profound lessons for magickal practitioners.

Magickal Applications of Dinosaur Energy

This book is your comprehensive guide to incorporating dinosaur energy into your magickal and spiritual practices. You'll learn to:

- Identify your personal dinosaur archetype or spirit guide.
- Create rituals and spells powered by the energy of specific dinosaurs.
- Build altars, sigils, and artifacts inspired by prehistoric magick.
- Harness fossils and other natural items as tools in your practice.
- Meditate with dinosaur energy for insight, courage, and transformation.

Each chapter focuses on a specific dinosaur or aspect of prehistoric magick, offering practical instructions, symbolic interpretations, and creative ways to integrate this energy into your daily life.

The Spiritual Legacy of Dinosaurs

While dinosaurs may seem like ancient relics of a distant past, their energy lives on. They remind us of the cyclical nature of life—birth, growth, dominance, and eventual transformation. They teach us about the power of adaptability, resilience in the face of change, and the importance of coexistence with the natural world.

By working with dinosaur energy, you'll not only enhance your magickal practice but also deepen your connection to the Earth and its history. You'll tap into a wellspring of primal power that can help you navigate life's challenges, achieve your goals, and embrace the ancient wisdom that still pulses beneath the surface of our modern world.

The Journey Ahead

As you embark on this journey, remember that dinosaur magick is as vast and diverse as the prehistoric world itself. The chapters ahead will provide you with the tools, insights, and inspiration needed to unlock the ancient magick of dinosaurs. Whether you are a seasoned magickal practitioner or a curious beginner, this guide offers something for everyone.

Prepare to step into a realm where ancient beasts once roamed and where their power still resonates. Let the dinosaurs be your allies, mentors, and sources of inspiration as you unlock the secrets of their ancient magick.

Welcome to **Dinosaurs of Power: Unlocking Ancient Magick.** The journey begins here.

Chapter 1: The Spiritual Connection to Dinosaurs

Dinosaurs, the titanic rulers of Earth's prehistoric past, continue to captivate our imaginations. Their fossilized remains are reminders of a world dominated by creatures whose size and power remain unparalleled. Beyond their physical existence, dinosaurs left an energetic and symbolic legacy that lingers in the spiritual and magickal realms. In this chapter, we will explore the profound connection between these ancient creatures and the spiritual world, uncovering the reasons why their energy still resonates and how it can be accessed in modern magick.

The Timeless Presence of Dinosaurs in Energy and Myth

Dinosaurs existed for over 165 million years, far longer than humans have walked the Earth. During their reign, they developed deep energetic ties to the planet, absorbing and influencing the Earth's natural energy cycles. These connections were not severed by their extinction but transformed into something more ethereal—a spiritual imprint that persists in the Earth's memory.

In many cultures, fossils and ancient bones have been considered sacred relics, imbued with the essence of life. In magick, such remnants are not just physical objects; they are repositories of power and wisdom. Dinosaurs, as beings who once dominated the Earth, carry a unique energetic frequency that resonates with themes of strength, survival, and transformation. Their energy can still be accessed today through intentional practices, meditations, and rituals.

The Symbolic Role of Dinosaurs in the Collective Unconscious

Dinosaurs hold a unique place in the collective unconscious of humanity. They are symbols of:

- **Power and Majesty:** Dinosaurs remind us of a time when raw, untamed power ruled the Earth. Their size and dominance make them archetypes of leadership and authority.
- **Survival and Adaptation:** Their long existence showcases the importance of adaptability and resilience. Even in extinction, their legacy remains, offering lessons in transformation and renewal.
- **Mystery and Discovery:** Dinosaurs symbolize the unknown and the thrill of uncovering hidden truths. They inspire exploration, curiosity, and a connection to Earth's mysteries.

These symbolic roles make dinosaurs ideal spiritual allies, capable of guiding us in areas where we seek strength, courage, and understanding.

The Energy Imprint of Dinosaurs

Just as humans leave energetic imprints in places they inhabit, dinosaurs left theirs in the Earth itself. This "energy fossil" is a spiritual record, much like the physical fossils that paleontologists uncover. This energetic presence can be accessed in specific ways:

1. **Through Fossils:** Fossils are direct connections to dinosaur energy. Holding or meditating with a fossil allows you to tap into the ancient vibrations of these creatures.
2. **Earth's Memory:** The Earth retains the energy of all life forms that have existed on it. Dinosaurs, as long-term inhabitants, left an especially potent imprint. You can connect with this energy by meditating in natural environments, particularly near fossil beds or ancient rock formations.
3. **Ancestral Spirits of the Earth:** Dinosaurs can be seen as ancestral spirits of the Earth, embodying its primal power and wisdom. Rituals honoring these spirits can unlock their guidance and protection.

Why Dinosaurs Resonate in the Spiritual Realm

Dinosaurs resonate in the spiritual realm because they represent archetypal forces that are universal and timeless. Unlike modern animals, which are tied to specific environments and roles, dinosaurs transcend these limitations. They are beings of myth and legend, allowing them to exist simultaneously in the realms of the physical, symbolic, and spiritual.

Additionally, their extinction adds a layer of mystique and spiritual power. The event that ended their reign symbolizes profound transformation—a cataclysmic change that paved the way for new life. This makes dinosaurs powerful symbols for rituals involving rebirth, renewal, and embracing change.

Accessing Dinosaur Energy in Modern Magick

Accessing dinosaur energy requires an understanding of their spiritual qualities and a willingness to engage with their primal essence. Here are some methods to begin connecting with their enduring presence:

1. Meditation and Visualization

Begin by visualizing the Earth during the Mesozoic Era. Imagine the lush forests, volcanic landscapes, and the thunderous footsteps of dinosaurs. Focus on the specific dinosaur whose energy you wish to connect with and invite its spirit to guide you. For example:

- Visualize the commanding presence of a Tyrannosaurus rex for courage and leadership.
- Picture the serene and grounded energy of a Brontosaurus for stability and peace.

2. Fossil Work and Sacred Tools

Fossils, whether real or symbolic, are powerful tools for accessing dinosaur energy. Incorporate them into your rituals, placing them on your altar or holding them during meditations. Fossils can amplify intentions, particularly for grounding, protection, and transformation spells.

3. Elemental Connections

Dinosaurs, as ancient beings, are deeply tied to the elements. You can use their energy in rituals by associating them with specific elements:

- **Fire:** Dinosaurs like the carnivorous T. rex embody the fierce and destructive power of fire.
- **Earth:** Herbivorous giants like Stegosaurus are deeply grounded, representing stability and abundance.
- **Air:** Flying dinosaurs like Pterodactyls connect to freedom and higher consciousness.
- **Water:** Dinosaurs that lived near aquatic environments symbolize adaptability and emotional balance.

4. Rituals and Offerings

Create rituals that honor the spirit of dinosaurs. Offer symbolic items like stones, feathers, or plants that represent prehistoric landscapes. Express gratitude for their energy and invite their guidance into your magickal workings.

Lessons from the Dinosaur Spirit

Dinosaurs teach us lessons that are just as relevant today as they were millions of years ago:

- **Resilience:** Their ability to adapt and thrive in diverse environments reminds us to remain flexible and resourceful.
- **Power:** Dinosaurs symbolize the importance of owning your strength and standing firm in the face of challenges.
- **Transformation:** Their extinction highlights the inevitability of change and the opportunity for renewal it brings.

By connecting with their energy, we can integrate these lessons into our lives, finding strength and inspiration in their ancient wisdom.

The Journey to Harnessing Dinosaur Energy

This chapter sets the foundation for your journey into dinosaur magick. By understanding their spiritual significance and learning how to access their energy, you are opening yourself to a world of untapped power. In the chapters ahead, you will delve deeper into specific dinosaurs, their archetypes, and the magickal practices that can bring their energy into your life.

The spiritual connection to dinosaurs is more than a fascination with the past; it is a profound opportunity to engage with the primal forces that shaped our world. As you embrace this connection, you'll discover a wellspring of magickal energy that will empower and transform your practice.

Chapter 2: Dinosaur Totems and Spirit Guides

In the vast and mysterious tapestry of spiritual practice, totems and spirit guides serve as conduits to powerful energies, archetypes, and lessons. Dinosaurs, as ancient creatures of immense presence, have the potential to act as some of the most potent and primal totems or spirit guides in your magickal journey. These prehistoric beings embody qualities such as resilience, strength, adaptability, and wisdom, making them invaluable allies for those seeking guidance, protection, or empowerment.

In this chapter, we will explore the concept of dinosaur totems and spirit guides, how to identify your personal dinosaur archetype, and the methods to connect with their energy through rituals and meditations.

What Are Totems and Spirit Guides?

A **totem** is a spiritual archetype or symbol that represents specific traits, energies, or life lessons. Totems often align with animals, plants, or other natural phenomena, acting as lifelong spiritual companions or temporary allies during specific phases of life.

A **spirit guide**, on the other hand, is a spiritual entity or consciousness that offers guidance, wisdom, and protection. Unlike totems, spirit guides may take on various forms and change as you grow spiritually.

Dinosaurs as totems or spirit guides bring an ancient and primal energy that connects deeply to the Earth's memory and its raw power. They offer a perspective rooted in endurance, survival, and the unyielding spirit of life.

Identifying Your Dinosaur Totem

Your dinosaur totem is the prehistoric archetype that resonates most closely with your personal energy, challenges, and aspirations. To discover your totem, reflect on the qualities you admire, the challenges you face, and the energies you seek to embody. Below are some common dinosaur archetypes and their spiritual attributes:

1. **Tyrannosaurus Rex (Power and Leadership)**
    - Symbolizes courage, dominance, and unyielding strength.
    - Ideal for those seeking to step into leadership roles or overcome fear.
2. **Velociraptor (Intelligence and Agility)**
    - Represents quick thinking, strategy, and adaptability.
    - A guide for those navigating complex situations or seeking mental clarity.
3. **Brontosaurus (Grounding and Stability)**
    - Embodies peace, patience, and grounded energy.
    - Perfect for those needing emotional balance and resilience.
4. **Pterodactyl (Freedom and Vision)**
    - Aligns with exploration, higher consciousness, and breaking free from constraints.
    - A totem for those yearning for independence or spiritual ascension.
5. **Stegosaurus (Protection and Boundaries)**
    - Symbolizes self-defense, resilience, and standing firm in one's beliefs.

- A guide for those working on creating healthy emotional or spiritual boundaries.
6. **Ankylosaurus (Fortification and Endurance)**
    - Represents protection, perseverance, and invulnerability.
    - Ideal for those needing strength during challenging times or shielding from negativity.
7. **Triceratops (Assertiveness and Harmony)**
    - Embodies balance between assertiveness and harmony.
    - A totem for those seeking to voice their truth while maintaining relationships.

Discovering Your Dinosaur Totem: A Guided Meditation

To find your dinosaur totem, perform the following meditation:

1. **Prepare Your Space:**
    - Find a quiet place where you won't be disturbed.
    - Light candles or incense that remind you of ancient forests or earthy tones, such as sandalwood or patchouli.
2. **Ground Yourself:**
    - Sit comfortably and take several deep breaths.
    - Visualize roots extending from your body into the Earth, grounding you in its ancient energy.
3. **Enter the Prehistoric World:**
    - Imagine the world millions of years ago, filled with lush greenery, towering trees, and the sounds of dinosaurs in the distance.
    - Picture yourself walking through this world, sensing its energy and life force.
4. **Call Forth Your Totem:**
    - As you walk, mentally or verbally state your intention: "I seek my dinosaur totem. Please reveal yourself to me."
    - Allow your mind to visualize or sense the presence of a dinosaur approaching.
5. **Connect with Your Totem:**
    - Observe the dinosaur. What species is it? How does it move? What energy does it project?
    - Ask it what lessons or guidance it has for you. Listen to its messages, whether through words, images, or feelings.
6. **Express Gratitude and Return:**
    - Thank your dinosaur totem for appearing.
    - Slowly return to your current awareness, bringing the energy and insights with you.

Working with Dinosaur Spirit Guides

Dinosaur spirit guides may come to you during specific periods of your life when their energy is most needed. Unlike totems, which are lifelong companions, spirit guides are more fluid and situational. They may manifest in dreams, meditations, or synchronicities.

Signs a Dinosaur Spirit Guide Is Present

- Recurring dreams or visions of a specific dinosaur.
- An unexplained fascination with a particular species.
- Emotional or intuitive sensations when encountering dinosaur imagery or fossils.

How to Call Upon a Dinosaur Spirit Guide

1. Create a sacred space and focus your intention.
2. Visualize the specific dinosaur you feel drawn to or its general energy.
3. Say aloud: "I call upon the spirit of [dinosaur species] to guide and assist me in my journey. Please share your wisdom and strength with me."

Incorporating Dinosaur Energy in Rituals

Once you've connected with your dinosaur totem or spirit guide, you can incorporate their energy into your magickal practices:

- **Altars:** Create a dinosaur-themed altar with fossils, figurines, or representations of your totem.
- **Sigils and Symbols:** Design sigils inspired by the shape, characteristics, or energy of your dinosaur.
- **Rituals:** Perform specific rituals invoking the strength, protection, or guidance of your dinosaur.
- **Daily Affirmations:** Use affirmations like, "With the courage of the Tyrannosaurus rex, I face my challenges boldly."

The Role of Dinosaur Totems in Magick

Dinosaur totems are powerful allies in both mundane and magickal pursuits. They can:

- Strengthen your resolve during difficult times.
- Protect you from negative energies.
- Guide you through transformations and personal growth.
- Enhance your ability to manifest your desires by channeling their primal energy.

Building a Lifelong Relationship

To deepen your bond with your dinosaur totem or spirit guide:

- Meditate regularly on their energy.
- Offer tokens of gratitude, such as natural items (stones, plants, or fossils).
- Reflect on their lessons and incorporate their traits into your daily life.

By nurturing this connection, you create a partnership with an ancient and potent force that can empower you in ways you never imagined.

Key Takeaways

- Dinosaur totems represent lifelong archetypes that align with your personal energy and goals.
- Spirit guides are more fluid and may appear during times of need.
- Use meditations, rituals, and altars to connect with and honor these prehistoric energies.
- By working with dinosaur totems and spirit guides, you can harness their ancient power to overcome challenges, grow spiritually, and manifest your desires.

Your journey with your dinosaur allies begins now. Let their ancient wisdom and raw strength guide you into a deeper connection with the Earth's primal forces.

Chapter 3: Harnessing the Primal Energy of Tyrannosaurus Rex

The **Tyrannosaurus rex**, the "king of the tyrant lizards," stands as one of the most iconic and fearsome creatures to have ever walked the Earth. Towering over its prey with immense power, sharp teeth, and an unrelenting drive, the T. rex embodies raw, unyielding strength, dominance, and survival. Harnessing its energy allows you to tap into unparalleled courage, personal protection, and the ability to assert yourself as a leader in any situation.

In this chapter, we will explore how to connect with the primal energy of the T. rex, its symbolic and spiritual meanings, and practical ways to channel its power into your life.

The Symbolism of Tyrannosaurus Rex

The T. rex is much more than a prehistoric predator—it is a powerful symbol of:

- **Courage:** The T. rex faced challenges head-on, thriving as an apex predator in a competitive ecosystem. Its energy instills bravery and fortitude to overcome fear.
- **Dominance:** As the ruler of its domain, the T. rex teaches us how to command respect, assert authority, and take control of our surroundings.
- **Survival:** Its relentless drive for survival reminds us of the importance of perseverance, adaptability, and resourcefulness in the face of adversity.
- **Protection:** With its immense size and strength, the T. rex inspires protective instincts, enabling you to defend yourself and others with confidence.

When you invoke the energy of the T. rex, you align yourself with these traits, empowering yourself to rise above challenges and assert your place in the world.

Connecting with the Energy of T. rex
Meditation for T. rex Energy

1. **Prepare Your Space:**
    - Choose a quiet, undisturbed area where you feel safe and grounded.
    - Surround yourself with items that evoke strength and primal energy, such as fossils, stones like obsidian or tiger's eye, or images of the T. rex.
2. **Ground Yourself:**
    - Sit or stand comfortably with your feet firmly planted on the ground.
    - Imagine roots growing from your body into the Earth, grounding you in its ancient energy.
3. **Visualize the T. rex:**
    - Close your eyes and picture a vast prehistoric landscape.
    - See a T. rex emerge, its footsteps shaking the ground, its presence commanding the environment.
4. **Invoke Its Energy:**
    - Imagine the T. rex noticing you and acknowledging your presence. Feel its power and strength flow into you, filling you with courage, protection, and dominance.
    - Repeat affirmations such as:

- "I embrace the courage and strength of the T. rex."
- "I stand tall, unyielding, and fearless."

5. **Integrate the Energy:**
    - As the meditation ends, visualize the T. rex's energy merging with your own, empowering you to face challenges and assert yourself with confidence.

Rituals for Harnessing T. rex Energy

1. Ritual for Courage

Use this ritual when you feel overwhelmed, uncertain, or in need of boldness.

- **Materials Needed:**
    - A red candle (symbolizing strength and courage)
    - A piece of tiger's eye or obsidian
    - A dinosaur figurine or an image of the T. rex
- **Steps:**
    - Light the red candle and place the stone and T. rex representation in front of you.
    - Focus on the candle's flame, imagining it as the burning heart of the T. rex.
    - Hold the stone in your hand and repeat:
      "Mighty T. rex, lend me your courage.
      Let me stand unyielding and brave,
      Fearless in the face of challenge."
    - Let the candle burn for a few moments as you absorb its energy, then extinguish it. Keep the stone with you as a talisman.

2. Protection Spell with T. rex Energy

Invoke the T. rex's protective instincts to create a spiritual shield around yourself or your loved ones.

- **Materials Needed:**
    - Black salt or a protective herb like sage
    - A drawing or carving of T. rex footprints
    - A small mirror
- **Steps:**
    - Create a circle of black salt around the area you wish to protect.
    - Place the mirror in the center, reflecting outward, symbolizing deflected negativity.
    - Place the T. rex footprints around the circle, calling on its strength to guard your space.
    - Chant:
      "Guardian of the ancient Earth,
      Protector of the primal lands,
      Stand as my shield, strong and true.
      No harm shall pass, no ill shall remain."

- Visualize a barrier forming around you, infused with the T. rex's unbreakable energy.

3. Spell for Dominance and Leadership

Perform this spell before situations requiring assertiveness or authority, such as interviews, presentations, or negotiations.

- **Materials Needed:**
    - A gold or bronze candle (symbolizing authority and success)
    - A feather or symbol of height and vision
    - A written intention (e.g., "I claim my rightful place as a leader")
- **Steps:**
    - Light the gold or bronze candle, focusing on its flame as a beacon of your rising power.
    - Hold the feather and visualize yourself standing tall, like the T. rex towering over its domain.
    - Speak your intention aloud, letting your voice carry the T. rex's commanding energy:
      "With the power of the Tyrannosaurus,
      I claim my strength, my vision, my throne.
      I lead with wisdom and unshakable force."
    - Burn the written intention in the candle flame, symbolizing its manifestation.

Incorporating T. rex Energy into Daily Life

- **Wear Dinosaur Symbolism:** Incorporate jewelry, clothing, or accessories featuring T. rex motifs to remind yourself of its power throughout the day.
- **Adopt a T. rex Affirmation:** Use daily affirmations like "I stand in my power, fearless and strong as the T. rex."
- **Visualize T. rex Power:** Before entering challenging situations, visualize the T. rex walking beside you, lending you its strength and confidence.

Key Lessons from T. rex Energy

The T. rex teaches us several key lessons for personal and spiritual growth:

- **Fearlessness:** Face challenges head-on, knowing you have the strength to overcome them.
- **Commanding Presence:** Step into leadership roles with confidence, commanding respect through your actions and words.
- **Persistence:** Even in adversity, channel the T. rex's relentless drive to survive and thrive.
- **Protection:** Guard what is important to you with unwavering strength and determination.

Embracing the Legacy of the T. rex

By connecting with the primal energy of the T. rex, you awaken a force within yourself that is both ancient and deeply empowering. This archetype of courage, dominance, and protection becomes a wellspring of strength that you can call upon whenever life demands boldness and resilience.

As you incorporate the T. rex's energy into your spiritual practice and daily life, you'll find yourself standing taller, speaking louder, and embracing challenges with unshakable confidence. This is the gift of the king of the tyrant lizards—a legacy of power that endures through the ages.

Chapter 4: The Graceful Strength of Brontosaurus

The **Brontosaurus**, or "thunder lizard," is a symbol of immense strength tempered by grace and serenity. Towering yet gentle, this herbivorous dinosaur moved with slow, deliberate purpose, embodying grounding, stability, and a deep connection to the Earth. Unlike the fierce and commanding Tyrannosaurus rex, the Brontosaurus represents a quiet strength that can weather storms, endure challenges, and provide an unshakable foundation in times of uncertainty.

In this chapter, you'll explore the spiritual and symbolic significance of the Brontosaurus, its role in magickal practices, and how to invoke its energy for stability, grounding, and inner peace.

The Symbolism of Brontosaurus

The Brontosaurus represents a unique blend of traits that are essential for personal growth and spiritual development. Its energy can be summarized through the following qualities:

1. **Strength Through Grace:** Though massive, the Brontosaurus was not aggressive. Its size alone was a defense, showing us that power can be gentle yet firm.
2. **Grounding and Stability:** As a creature that roamed vast plains, the Brontosaurus maintained a steady connection to the Earth, offering lessons in staying grounded and centered.
3. **Patience and Endurance:** Moving slowly and deliberately, the Brontosaurus teaches us the value of persistence and the strength found in measured action.
4. **Community and Protection:** Often moving in herds, this dinosaur embodies the importance of unity, cooperation, and providing security to those around you.

Harnessing the energy of the Brontosaurus allows you to embody these traits, creating a foundation of stability and peace in your life while fostering resilience and connection.

The Spiritual Lessons of Brontosaurus

The Brontosaurus energy offers profound spiritual lessons that can guide you through life's challenges:

- **Anchor Yourself in Turmoil:** When chaos arises, the Brontosaurus teaches you to remain steady, allowing the storm to pass without being uprooted.
- **Find Strength in Slowness:** In a world that glorifies speed and urgency, the Brontosaurus reminds you to embrace deliberate, purposeful movement.
- **Connect Deeply with the Earth:** This dinosaur's strong connection to the ground symbolizes the importance of staying rooted in your values, community, and natural surroundings.
- **Balance Strength and Gentleness:** True power doesn't always roar—it can move quietly yet make an indelible impact.

Meditation to Connect with Brontosaurus Energy

Meditation is a powerful way to channel the grounding and stabilizing energy of the Brontosaurus. Follow this guided meditation to attune yourself to its essence:

1. **Prepare Your Space:**
    - Find a quiet space where you won't be disturbed.
    - Use earthy elements, such as green and brown candles, stones like jasper or hematite, and soft, grounding scents like cedarwood or sandalwood.
2. **Ground Yourself:**
    - Sit or lie down in a comfortable position.
    - Visualize roots growing from your body into the Earth, connecting you deeply to its energy.
3. **Enter the Prehistoric World:**
    - Imagine yourself standing on a lush, prehistoric plain under a wide-open sky. Feel the Earth beneath your feet, steady and unyielding.
    - Visualize a Brontosaurus emerging from the horizon, moving with slow, deliberate grace.
4. **Absorb Its Energy:**
    - As the Brontosaurus approaches, sense its calm, grounding presence enveloping you.
    - Imagine its strength flowing into you, anchoring you to the Earth and filling you with peace and stability.
5. **Receive Guidance:**
    - Ask the Brontosaurus what wisdom it has to offer. Listen for any messages or impressions.
6. **Express Gratitude:**
    - Thank the Brontosaurus for sharing its energy and wisdom.
    - Slowly return to your awareness, feeling grounded and renewed.

Rituals for Grounding and Stability
1. Grounding Ritual with Brontosaurus Energy
Use this ritual to reconnect with the Earth and find stability during times of upheaval.

- **Materials Needed:**
    - A piece of jasper or hematite (grounding stones)
    - A bowl of soil or Earth
    - A green candle
- **Steps:**
    - Place the bowl of soil on your altar or sacred space.
    - Light the green candle and hold the stone in your hand.
    - Visualize the Brontosaurus, feeling its grounding energy surround you.
    - Say aloud:
      "Mighty Brontosaurus, anchor of the Earth,
      Teach me your strength, your patience, your calm.
      Root me in stability, shield me from harm.
      I walk with steady steps, unshaken and strong."
    - Bury the stone in the soil as a symbolic act of grounding your energy.

2. Ritual for Inner Peace
This ritual helps you release stress and embrace tranquility.

- **Materials Needed:**
    - A white or pale blue candle
    - Lavender or chamomile incense
    - A bowl of water
- **Steps:**
    - Light the candle and incense, creating a serene atmosphere.
    - Place your hands over the bowl of water and visualize it as a pool of calm energy.
    - Picture the Brontosaurus moving slowly and peacefully, its energy radiating calm.
    - Dip your fingers into the water and gently touch your forehead, heart, and hands, saying:
      "Brontosaurus, guide me to peace.
      Wash away my worry, grant me release.
      With your grace, I find my calm,
      A steady heart, a soothing balm."

Incorporating Brontosaurus Energy into Daily Life

- **Embrace Slow Living:** Take inspiration from the Brontosaurus by practicing patience and mindfulness. Focus on the present moment rather than rushing toward the future.
- **Strengthen Your Foundations:** Build habits, routines, and relationships that provide stability and support, much like the Brontosaurus relied on its herd and the Earth beneath it.
- **Use Grounding Stones:** Carry stones like hematite, jasper, or smoky quartz to maintain a sense of grounding throughout the day.
- **Visualize Brontosaurus Power:** In moments of stress, visualize the Brontosaurus walking beside you, its steady energy calming and centering you.

Key Lessons from Brontosaurus Energy

The Brontosaurus teaches several vital lessons that can enhance your spiritual and magickal practice:

- **Strength is Gentle:** True power doesn't always need to assert itself aggressively; quiet confidence can be just as effective.
- **Stay Grounded:** In times of chaos, remain connected to your foundation and values.
- **Move with Purpose:** Slow, deliberate action often leads to more sustainable outcomes than impulsive decisions.
- **Foster Community:** Like the Brontosaurus moving in herds, seek connection and support from others to enhance your resilience.

The Legacy of the Brontosaurus

The Brontosaurus represents the kind of strength that doesn't falter or waver, a quiet resilience that holds firm no matter the circumstances. Its energy teaches us to stand tall, remain steady, and move through life with deliberate grace.

By incorporating the wisdom of the Brontosaurus into your spiritual practice, you can cultivate a sense of inner peace, stability, and unwavering strength that will empower you in every aspect of your life. As you journey forward, let the Brontosaurus serve as a gentle yet powerful guide, anchoring you in the strength of the Earth and the serenity of its timeless presence.

Chapter 5: Velociraptor Magick: Precision and Speed

The **Velociraptor**, with its speed, agility, and razor-sharp intellect, symbolizes mastery over precision and adaptability. Unlike the towering giants of its era, the Velociraptor thrived not through brute strength but through strategic thinking, clever tactics, and swift action. In magickal practice, the energy of the Velociraptor can be harnessed to enhance mental clarity, quick decision-making, and adaptability in the face of change or challenges.

In this chapter, you will learn how to tap into the sharp, agile energy of the Velociraptor to empower your mind and actions, making you a more effective problem-solver, strategist, and practitioner of magick.

The Symbolism of the Velociraptor

The Velociraptor is often associated with the following traits:

1. **Sharp Intellect:** Known for its cunning, the Velociraptor represents mental clarity, problem-solving, and intellectual sharpness.
2. **Agility and Speed:** Its quick, precise movements make it a symbol of adaptability and efficiency.
3. **Strategic Thinking:** The Velociraptor's ability to hunt in packs and employ clever tactics mirrors the importance of planning and collaboration.
4. **Focus and Precision:** Its laser-focused approach to hunting teaches us to direct energy and attention toward specific goals without distraction.
5. **Survival through Adaptation:** Thriving in varied environments, the Velociraptor embodies the ability to adapt quickly to changing circumstances.

These qualities make Velociraptor energy invaluable for navigating complex situations, overcoming challenges, and excelling in both mundane and magickal pursuits.

Harnessing Velociraptor Energy for Mental Clarity and Quick Decision-Making

When life demands quick thinking and adaptability, channeling Velociraptor energy can help sharpen your focus and guide your decisions. Here are some practical steps to align with this dynamic energy:

1. Velociraptor Meditation for Mental Clarity

This meditation is designed to sharpen your intellect and bring clarity to your thoughts.

1. **Prepare Your Space:**
    - Use candles in shades of silver or blue to symbolize clarity and intellect.
    - Place symbols of agility, such as feathers or sleek stones like fluorite or clear quartz, on your altar.
2. **Visualize the Velociraptor:**
    - Close your eyes and imagine a lush prehistoric forest.
    - Picture a Velociraptor moving gracefully through the terrain, its keen eyes scanning for opportunities.
3. **Invite Its Energy:**
    - As you observe the Velociraptor, invite its energy to flow into you. Visualize its sharp mind and swift movements becoming part of your own abilities.
4. **Focus on Your Goal:**
    - Hold a specific question or situation in your mind. Allow the clarity and decisiveness of the Velociraptor to guide your thoughts and offer solutions.
5. **End with Gratitude:**
    - Thank the Velociraptor for its guidance and carry its energy with you throughout the day.

2. Quick Decision-Making Ritual

When faced with a challenging decision, use this ritual to invoke Velociraptor energy for swift and accurate resolution.

- **Materials Needed:**
    - A silver or yellow candle (symbolizing speed and intellect)
    - A piece of fluorite or clear quartz
    - A small piece of paper and a pen
- **Steps:**
    - Light the candle and hold the fluorite or quartz in your hand.
    - Write your dilemma or decision on the piece of paper.
    - Say aloud:
      "Velociraptor, swift and wise,
      Lend your focus to my eyes.

> Help me see, help me know,
> The path to take, the way to go."
- Burn the paper in the candle flame, visualizing your decision becoming clear.
- Keep the crystal with you as a reminder of your focus and resolve.

Adaptability and Strategic Thinking

The Velociraptor's ability to adapt quickly to changing environments and strategize in its hunts offers valuable lessons for navigating complex situations.

Adapting to Change with Velociraptor Energy

Change is a constant in life, and the Velociraptor teaches us to thrive in its presence. When adapting to new circumstances:

1. **Pause and Assess:** Take a moment to observe your surroundings and understand the changes, just as the Velociraptor surveys its environment before making a move.
2. **Focus on Strengths:** Identify your strengths and use them strategically to navigate the situation.
3. **Move Quickly but Deliberately:** Avoid hesitation, but ensure each action is purposeful and directed toward your goals.

Magickal Practices for Precision

1. Focus Spell with Velociraptor Energy

Use this spell when you need to concentrate on a specific task or goal.

- **Materials Needed:**
    - A blue candle
    - A small mirror
    - A sharp object (symbolic, such as a needle or a knife)
- **Steps:**
    - Light the blue candle and place the mirror in front of it.
    - Hold the sharp object and reflect its image in the mirror, symbolizing clarity and precision.
    - Say:
      "With the focus of Velociraptor's sight,
      I direct my energy, sharp and bright.
      Distractions fade, my goal is clear,
      My path is true, my success is near."
    - Meditate on the flame for a few moments, visualizing your goal with perfect clarity.

2. Enhanced Agility Ritual

To improve your physical or mental agility, call upon the swift and adaptable energy of the Velociraptor.

- **Materials Needed:**
  - A feather (symbolizing agility)
  - A yellow candle
  - A piece of citrine or clear quartz
- **Steps:**
  - Light the yellow candle and place the feather and stone in front of it.
  - Hold the feather and visualize yourself moving gracefully and quickly, overcoming obstacles with ease.
  - Say:
    "Velociraptor, nimble and wise,
    Lend me your speed beneath open skies.
    My steps are swift, my mind is clear,
    With your grace, no challenge I fear."
  - Carry the feather or stone with you as a talisman.

Incorporating Velociraptor Energy in Daily Life

- **Quick Thinking:** When faced with sudden challenges, pause and visualize the Velociraptor's agility and decisiveness guiding you to the right action.
- **Strategic Planning:** Approach problems like a Velociraptor—analyze your situation, plan your moves, and execute them with precision.
- **Stay Agile:** Be open to changes in plans and willing to pivot quickly when necessary.

Key Lessons from Velociraptor Energy

The Velociraptor offers essential lessons for personal and magickal growth:

- **Clarity of Thought:** Sharpen your mind and focus on what truly matters.
- **Adaptability:** Learn to thrive in dynamic and changing environments.
- **Precision and Action:** Approach goals with purpose and execute plans with efficiency.
- **Collaborative Strength:** Recognize the power of teamwork and strategic alliances.

The Legacy of the Velociraptor

The Velociraptor, though small compared to its prehistoric peers, wielded unmatched agility and intellect to dominate its environment. Its energy teaches us that success often comes not from brute force but from cleverness, adaptability, and precision.

By incorporating the energy of the Velociraptor into your spiritual practice and daily life, you can navigate challenges with sharp intellect, execute plans with agility, and achieve your goals with unwavering focus. Let the Velociraptor inspire you to move through life with speed, precision, and a mind as sharp as its claws.

Chapter 6: Pterodactyl's Sky Magick

The **Pterodactyl**, a master of the skies during the prehistoric era, embodies the essence of freedom, perspective, and ascension. Though not technically a dinosaur, this winged reptile was one of the first creatures to conquer the air, symbolizing the human desire to rise above earthly constraints. In magick, the energy of the Pterodactyl can be harnessed for astral travel, dream work, gaining higher perspectives, and casting spells for freedom and liberation.

In this chapter, you will learn how to tap into the ethereal qualities of the Pterodactyl to expand your spiritual practice, connect with higher realms, and manifest a sense of boundless freedom.

The Symbolism of the Pterodactyl

The Pterodactyl's unique characteristics make it a powerful archetype in magickal work. Its symbolism includes:

1. **Freedom and Liberation:** As a creature of the skies, the Pterodactyl represents breaking free from limitations, whether physical, emotional, or spiritual.
2. **Higher Perspective:** Flying high above the Earth, it offers clarity and insight, enabling you to see the bigger picture.
3. **Ascension and Spiritual Connection:** The Pterodactyl's connection to the air element makes it a guide for accessing higher planes and realms.
4. **Agility and Grace:** Its ability to navigate the air teaches adaptability and fluidity in thought and action.
5. **Dream and Vision Work:** As a creature associated with the skies, it naturally lends itself to dream magick and astral exploration.

These qualities make the Pterodactyl an invaluable guide for those seeking to expand their consciousness, gain clarity, or work toward personal freedom.

Pterodactyl Magick: Areas of Practice

Pterodactyl magick is versatile and can be applied in various areas of spiritual and magickal practice:

1. **Astral Travel:** Use its energy to navigate the astral plane with grace and safety.
2. **Dream Work:** Enhance your ability to lucid dream, interpret dreams, and use dreams for spiritual growth.
3. **Freedom Spells:** Break free from constraints, such as limiting beliefs, toxic relationships, or oppressive situations.
4. **Perspective Shifts:** Gain clarity and a broader view of complex situations.
5. **Connection to Air Element:** Incorporate the qualities of air—intellect, communication, and inspiration—into your practice.

Connecting with Pterodactyl Energy
To work with Pterodactyl energy, you must attune yourself to its airy and ascendant qualities.
1. Meditation to Connect with the Pterodactyl

1. **Prepare Your Space:**
    - Use light, airy colors like white, pale blue, or silver in your space.
    - Light incense or essential oils associated with air, such as frankincense, lavender, or peppermint.
2. **Ground Yourself:**
    - Sit comfortably and visualize roots anchoring you to the Earth. Even as you prepare to soar, grounding ensures you can return safely.
3. **Visualize the Pterodactyl:**
    - Imagine a vast prehistoric sky. See a Pterodactyl gliding effortlessly through the air, its wings spread wide.
    - Picture yourself joining it, either riding on its back or flying alongside it.
4. **Feel Its Energy:**
    - Sense the freedom, weightlessness, and boundless perspective that come with soaring through the sky.
    - Allow the Pterodactyl to share its wisdom, guidance, or messages with you.
5. **Return to the Ground:**
    - When ready, thank the Pterodactyl for its presence and guidance. Gently return to your awareness, bringing its energy with you.

Rituals for Pterodactyl Magick

1. Astral Travel Ritual

Harness Pterodactyl energy to explore the astral plane safely and effectively.

- **Materials Needed:**
    - A feather or wing-shaped object
    - A silver or white candle
    - Lavender or frankincense incense
- **Steps:**
    - Light the candle and incense, creating a calm and focused atmosphere.
    - Hold the feather or wing-shaped object in your hands, visualizing it as your connection to the Pterodactyl's energy.
    - Say:
    "Pterodactyl, master of flight,
    Guide me through the astral night.
    With your wings, I safely soar,
    To realms unseen, through spirit's door."
    - Lie down and focus on your breath, imagining yourself lifting from your body and soaring through the skies with the Pterodactyl.
    - Upon returning, ground yourself by touching the Earth or holding a grounding stone like hematite.

2. Freedom Spell

Use this spell to break free from constraints and reclaim your sense of independence.

- **Materials Needed:**
    - A blue candle (symbolizing freedom and clarity)
    - A piece of amethyst or aquamarine
    - A small piece of paper and a pen
- **Steps:**
    - Write down the situation or belief you wish to be freed from on the piece of paper.
    - Light the blue candle and hold the stone in your hand.
    - Say:
    "Pterodactyl, soaring high,
    Lift my spirit to the sky.
    Break these chains, set me free,
    Wings of freedom, carry me."
    - Burn the paper in the candle flame, visualizing the constraints dissolving into smoke.
    - Keep the stone as a reminder of your liberation.

3. Dream Work Ritual
Enhance your dreams and open the gateway to deeper insights with Pterodactyl energy.

- **Materials Needed:**
    - A small dream journal
    - A light blue candle
    - Mugwort or chamomile tea
- **Steps:**
    - Before bed, light the candle and sip the tea while setting the intention to remember and interpret your dreams.
    - Say:
    "Pterodactyl of the dreamtime sky,
    Bring me visions as I fly.
    Through the night, let wisdom flow,
    Secrets revealed, truths I'll know."
    - Place the candle on a safe surface and let it burn while you fall asleep. Keep the dream journal nearby to record your dreams upon waking.

Incorporating Pterodactyl Energy into Daily Life

- **Perspective Practices:** When faced with challenges, visualize the Pterodactyl soaring above the situation, helping you see the broader picture.
- **Freedom Affirmations:** Use affirmations like "I am free to rise above all that holds me back" to align with Pterodactyl energy.
- **Air Element Correspondences:** Incorporate symbols of air, such as feathers, wind chimes, or light stones like selenite, into your surroundings.

Key Lessons from Pterodactyl Energy
The Pterodactyl offers profound spiritual lessons, including:

1. **The Power of Freedom:** Embrace liberation from limiting beliefs, situations, or mindsets.
2. **Perspective Matters:** A higher vantage point often reveals solutions and opportunities unseen from the ground.
3. **Fluidity and Grace:** Move through life with agility and ease, adapting to changes as they arise.
4. **Connection to Higher Realms:** Open yourself to messages and insights from spiritual realms, trusting the guidance of the Pterodactyl.

The Legacy of the Pterodactyl

The Pterodactyl's mastery of the skies represents our own potential to rise above earthly constraints and connect with higher realms of consciousness. Its energy teaches us to embrace freedom, seek clarity, and move through life with the grace of a creature born to soar.

By integrating Pterodactyl magick into your practice, you open the door to boundless possibilities, enabling you to explore new dimensions, gain profound insights, and reclaim your inherent right to live a life unburdened and free. Let the Pterodactyl's wings carry you to new heights, where your spirit can truly thrive.

Chapter 7: Stegosaurus as a Symbol of Defense and Resilience

The **Stegosaurus**, with its iconic plates and spiked tail, represents a profound balance of defense and gentleness. Though a peaceful herbivore, the Stegosaurus was well-equipped to protect itself against predators, embodying resilience, self-defense, and the power to stand firm in the face of adversity. As a spiritual ally, the Stegosaurus offers protective energy to shield you from negativity and fortify your emotional and spiritual boundaries.

In this chapter, you will learn how to harness the energy of the Stegosaurus to build resilience, protect your aura, and establish a strong, unwavering sense of self.

The Symbolism of the Stegosaurus

The Stegosaurus is a powerful symbol in magick, representing key traits that are essential for self-protection and emotional strength:

1. **Defense and Protection:** The Stegosaurus's spiked tail, or thagomizer, is a reminder of the importance of guarding oneself against external threats.
2. **Resilience:** Despite its seemingly gentle nature, the Stegosaurus was a survivor, thriving in a dangerous prehistoric world.
3. **Boundaries:** Its plated back acts as a shield, symbolizing the need for strong boundaries to protect your energy and emotions.
4. **Balance:** The Stegosaurus teaches the harmony between strength and vulnerability, showing that resilience doesn't mean aggression but the ability to stand firm when needed.
5. **Grounding and Stability:** As a creature deeply connected to the Earth, the Stegosaurus represents grounding energy that helps you remain centered in challenging times.

These qualities make the Stegosaurus an ideal ally for shielding yourself from negativity, toxic influences, and emotional drain.

The Spiritual Lessons of the Stegosaurus

The Stegosaurus teaches profound lessons that are essential for emotional and spiritual growth:

- **Stand Your Ground:** Know when to assert your boundaries and protect your space.
- **Guard Your Energy:** Not every situation or person deserves your time and energy. The Stegosaurus reminds you to conserve your resources for what truly matters.
- **Balance Vulnerability and Strength:** You don't need to be aggressive to be strong; sometimes, quiet resilience is the greatest form of defense.
- **Adaptation and Survival:** Resilience comes from learning how to adapt to challenges while maintaining your core identity.

Harnessing Stegosaurus Energy for Protection and Resilience
1. Meditation to Connect with Stegosaurus Energy

Meditation is a powerful way to attune yourself to the protective and grounding energy of the Stegosaurus.

1. **Prepare Your Space:**
    - Use earthy tones like green, brown, or orange in your space.
    - Incorporate grounding scents such as cedarwood, patchouli, or vetiver.
2. **Ground Yourself:**
    - Sit comfortably and imagine roots extending from your body deep into the Earth. Feel the stability and strength of the ground beneath you.
3. **Visualize the Stegosaurus:**
    - Picture a serene prehistoric landscape. See a Stegosaurus grazing peacefully but alert, its plates and tail ready to defend if necessary.
    - Imagine the Stegosaurus approaching you, its energy surrounding you like an impenetrable shield.
4. **Absorb Its Energy:**
    - Visualize the plates of the Stegosaurus forming a protective barrier around you, deflecting negativity and harmful energy.
    - Feel its resilience infusing your spirit, fortifying your boundaries and emotional strength.
5. **Express Gratitude:**
    - Thank the Stegosaurus for sharing its energy and wisdom. Carry its lessons with you as you move through your day.

2. Shielding Ritual with Stegosaurus Energy

Use this ritual to create a powerful energetic shield that protects you from negativity and toxic influences.

- **Materials Needed:**
    - A green or brown candle
    - A piece of black tourmaline or obsidian (for protection)
    - A bowl of salt or Earth
- **Steps:**
    - Light the candle and place the stone and bowl of salt/Earth in front of you.
    - Visualize the Stegosaurus standing beside you, its plates forming a barrier around your aura.
    - Say:
      "Guardian of ancient Earth,
      Shield me with your steadfast worth.
      Plates of steel, tail of might,
      Protect my soul, day and night."
    - Hold the stone in your hand, imagining it absorbing and neutralizing all negativity around you.
    - Scatter the salt or Earth around your space as a physical manifestation of your shield.

3. Ritual for Strengthening Emotional Boundaries

This ritual helps reinforce your emotional boundaries and prevent energy drain from toxic relationships or environments.

- **Materials Needed:**
    - A piece of jasper or hematite
    - A piece of paper and pen
    - A red or orange candle
- **Steps:**
    - Write down any situations or relationships that feel overwhelming or draining.
    - Light the candle and hold the jasper or hematite in your hand.
    - Visualize the Stegosaurus standing between you and the source of emotional strain, its plates deflecting any harmful energy.
    - Say:
      "Stegosaurus, defender of peace,
      Let your strength grant me release.
      Guard my heart, protect my mind,
      With your resilience, I draw the line."
    - Burn the paper in the candle flame, symbolizing the release of these draining influences.

Daily Practices for Incorporating Stegosaurus Energy

- **Visualize Plates of Protection:** Before entering challenging situations, imagine the plates of a Stegosaurus forming a shield around you, reflecting negativity away.
- **Carry a Protective Stone:** Keep stones like black tourmaline, hematite, or jasper with you as talismans of defense and resilience.
- **Use Affirmations:** Repeat affirmations like "I am strong, grounded, and protected. My boundaries are sacred and unbreakable."
- **Practice Grounding Exercises:** Spend time in nature, walk barefoot on the Earth, or meditate with grounding stones to maintain a strong connection to your inner stability.

Key Lessons from Stegosaurus Energy

The Stegosaurus imparts several vital lessons for building resilience and maintaining protection:

1. **Strength is Quiet but Firm:** You don't need to be aggressive to protect yourself. Quiet resilience is often the most effective form of defense.
2. **Boundaries Are Essential:** Establishing and maintaining boundaries is an act of self-care and respect.
3. **Ground Yourself:** Staying connected to your inner strength and the Earth helps you remain calm and centered in any situation.
4. **Be Prepared but Peaceful:** Like the Stegosaurus, move through life peacefully, but always be ready to defend yourself when necessary.

The Legacy of the Stegosaurus

The Stegosaurus, with its gentle nature and formidable defenses, serves as a reminder that true strength lies in balance. Its energy teaches us to embrace our vulnerabilities while fortifying ourselves against harm. By invoking the Stegosaurus, you gain a powerful ally in shielding your energy, protecting your spirit, and fostering resilience in the face of adversity.

Incorporating the wisdom and power of the Stegosaurus into your spiritual practice empowers you to walk through life with quiet confidence, unshakable boundaries, and the knowledge that you are fully protected. Let the Stegosaurus be your guardian, guiding you toward a life of peace, strength, and resilience.

Chapter 8: Triceratops: The Horned Guardian

The **Triceratops**, with its iconic three horns and robust frill, embodies the archetype of a protective guardian and a force of assertive strength. While a peaceful herbivore by nature, this prehistoric titan was well-equipped to defend itself and its herd from predators, symbolizing the power of standing firm and using your voice to assert your will. The Triceratops energy offers a unique blend of protection, courage, and assertiveness, making it a potent ally in overcoming challenges, speaking your truth, and safeguarding your personal boundaries.

In this chapter, you will explore the magickal and spiritual qualities of the Triceratops, how to invoke its energy for protection and self-expression, and practical rituals to channel its horned guardian power.

The Symbolism of the Triceratops

The Triceratops carries profound symbolic meanings that resonate with both strength and stability:

1. **Defense and Protection:** Its horns and frill represent a natural barrier against threats, symbolizing the ability to guard oneself and others.
2. **Assertiveness:** The Triceratops's horns are a metaphor for confidently asserting your will and standing up for what you believe in.
3. **Community and Leadership:** Often found in herds, the Triceratops symbolizes unity and the protective role of a leader or guardian.
4. **Grounded Strength:** Despite its size and power, the Triceratops remained grounded and connected to the Earth, teaching resilience and steadfastness.
5. **Balanced Energy:** Its peaceful nature, paired with its readiness to defend when necessary, demonstrates the importance of balancing calmness with assertive action.

By working with Triceratops energy, you can enhance your ability to protect yourself, confidently express your needs, and lead with integrity.

The Spiritual Lessons of the Triceratops

The Triceratops teaches several key spiritual lessons that can enhance your personal growth and magickal practice:

- **Stand Your Ground:** When faced with challenges, the Triceratops reminds you to hold firm and not back down in the face of adversity.
- **Speak with Confidence:** Its horns symbolize the power of clear and assertive communication.
- **Lead with Courage:** The Triceratops energy encourages you to protect and support those in your care.
- **Balance Action and Peace:** Learn when to act decisively and when to remain calm, maintaining harmony between these two states.

Connecting with Triceratops Energy

To tap into the protective and assertive qualities of the Triceratops, you must align yourself with its grounded yet powerful energy.

1. Meditation to Embody the Horned Guardian

1. **Prepare Your Space:**
    - Use earthy tones like green and brown to decorate your space.
    - Light grounding scents such as sandalwood, cedar, or patchouli.
    - Include a triangular object (representing the Triceratops's three horns) as a focal point.
2. **Ground Yourself:**
    - Sit comfortably with your feet planted firmly on the ground.
    - Visualize roots growing from your body into the Earth, anchoring you in stability.
3. **Visualize the Triceratops:**
    - Picture a vast prehistoric plain. A Triceratops emerges, standing tall and confident, its horns gleaming in the sunlight.
    - Feel its protective and assertive energy surrounding you.
4. **Absorb Its Strength:**
    - Imagine its horns transferring energy to you, filling you with courage and confidence.
    - Envision its frill forming a shield around you, protecting you from harm and negativity.
5. **End with Gratitude:**
    - Thank the Triceratops for sharing its energy and carry its lessons with you as you return to your day.

Rituals for Protection and Assertion

1. Protective Shield Ritual

This ritual creates a spiritual shield using Triceratops energy to guard against negativity or harmful influences.

- **Materials Needed:**
    - A triangular stone (e.g., jasper or obsidian)
    - A green candle
    - A small bowl of salt
- **Steps:**
    - Light the green candle and place the stone in front of you.
    - Sprinkle salt in a circle around your space, visualizing it as a barrier of protection.
    - Hold the stone and say:
      "Triceratops, horned guardian true,
      Shield me now with strength from you.
      Your frill deflects all harm away,
      Your courage guides me through the day."
    - Visualize a translucent shield forming around you, strong and impenetrable.

- Place the stone in your pocket or on your altar as a symbol of ongoing protection.

2. Ritual for Assertive Communication

When you need to speak your truth or assert yourself, this ritual helps amplify your voice with the strength of the Triceratops.

- **Materials Needed:**
    - A blue candle (symbolizing communication)
    - A clear quartz crystal (to amplify energy)
    - A piece of paper and a pen
- **Steps:**
    - Light the blue candle and hold the quartz crystal in your hand.
    - Write down what you need to communicate, focusing on clarity and honesty.
    - Say aloud:
      "Mighty Triceratops, lend me your voice,
      To speak with courage, to make my choice.
      With your strength, my words are clear,
      Assertive, true, and without fear."
    - Burn the paper in the candle flame, releasing your intention to the universe.
    - Carry the quartz crystal with you as a talisman for confident communication.

3. Empowerment Spell for Leadership

This spell draws on the Triceratops's protective and unifying energy to help you step into leadership roles with courage and integrity.

- **Materials Needed:**
    - A gold or yellow candle
    - A piece of citrine or tiger's eye
    - A symbol of your leadership goal (e.g., a key, a badge, or a written affirmation)
- **Steps:**
    - Light the gold or yellow candle and place the symbol and stone before it.
    - Visualize the Triceratops leading its herd, confident and strong. Imagine yourself embodying the same qualities.
    - Say:
      "Guardian Triceratops, strong and wise,
      Guide me as I lead and rise.
      With courage true and steady will,
      Help me lead with strength and skill."
    - Hold the stone and the symbol together, infusing them with your intention.
    - Keep the symbol in a visible place as a reminder of your leadership goals.

Incorporating Triceratops Energy in Daily Life

- **Visualize Its Strength:** Before entering challenging situations, imagine the Triceratops walking beside you, its horns ready to defend and its frill shielding you from harm.
- **Wear Symbols of Protection:** Use jewelry or accessories featuring triangular shapes to invoke the Triceratops's protective energy.
- **Set Boundaries with Confidence:** When saying no or establishing limits, channel the Triceratops's assertive energy to stand firm in your decisions.
- **Practice Daily Affirmations:** Repeat affirmations such as, "I stand strong, protected and confident. My voice is powerful, and my boundaries are respected."

Key Lessons from Triceratops Energy

The Triceratops imparts vital lessons for personal empowerment and resilience:

1. **Protection Comes from Confidence:** You can guard yourself effectively by being assertive and standing your ground.
2. **Voice Your Truth:** Speak honestly and clearly, even in challenging situations.
3. **Balance Peace and Defense:** Be calm and grounded, but ready to act when necessary.
4. **Lead with Integrity:** Protect and guide others with courage and compassion.

The Legacy of the Triceratops

The Triceratops, with its iconic horns and steadfast nature, serves as a reminder of the strength found in balance. Its energy empowers you to protect yourself and others, assert your will, and confidently navigate life's challenges.

By incorporating Triceratops energy into your magickal and daily practices, you can cultivate resilience, strengthen your boundaries, and lead with courage and integrity. Let the Triceratops inspire you to stand tall as a horned guardian of your own life, embracing the power to protect and the courage to thrive.

Chapter 9: Ankylosaurus and Magickal Fortification

The **Ankylosaurus**, often referred to as the "armored tank" of the prehistoric world, is a powerful symbol of protection, resilience, and steadfastness. With its heavily armored body and formidable club-like tail, the Ankylosaurus represents an impenetrable defense against external threats. In magickal practice, invoking the energy of the Ankylosaurus can help you create a spiritual armor, fortify your defenses, and establish an unshakable foundation for your magickal workings.

In this chapter, you will delve into the symbolism and spiritual significance of the Ankylosaurus, learn how to harness its protective energies, and explore practical rituals and meditations to build your own magickal fortification.

The Symbolism of the Ankylosaurus

The Ankylosaurus embodies several key qualities that are invaluable in both magickal practice and personal development:

1. **Protection and Defense:** With its armored plates and defensive tail, the Ankylosaurus is a symbol of ultimate protection against harm.
2. **Resilience and Endurance:** Its ability to withstand attacks without faltering represents inner strength and the capacity to endure challenges.
3. **Grounded Stability:** As a creature firmly connected to the Earth, it signifies stability and grounding, essential for any magickal foundation.
4. **Immovable Presence:** The Ankylosaurus teaches us to stand firm in our beliefs and maintain our position despite external pressures.
5. **Fortification of Boundaries:** Its physical armor reflects the importance of establishing and maintaining strong personal and spiritual boundaries.

By aligning with the Ankylosaurus's energy, you can build a protective barrier around your spiritual practice, ensuring that negative influences and energies are kept at bay.

The Spiritual Lessons of the Ankylosaurus

The Ankylosaurus offers profound spiritual insights that can enhance your magickal journey:

- **Building Strong Foundations:** Just as its armor is built from interlocking plates, your magickal practice should be built on a solid, interconnected foundation of knowledge, discipline, and intention.
- **Creating Spiritual Armor:** Learn to shield yourself from negativity, psychic attacks, and energy drain through visualization and protective rituals.
- **Resilience in Adversity:** The Ankylosaurus teaches the importance of resilience, encouraging you to remain steadfast in the face of challenges.
- **Establishing Boundaries:** Recognize the necessity of setting clear boundaries in both the physical and spiritual realms to protect your well-being.

Connecting with Ankylosaurus Energy

To harness the protective and grounding energies of the Ankylosaurus, you can engage in specific meditations and rituals designed to align your spirit with this ancient guardian.

1. Meditation for Spiritual Armor

This meditation helps you visualize and build your own spiritual armor inspired by the Ankylosaurus's protective plates.

1. **Prepare Your Space:**
    - Choose a quiet, comfortable area where you won't be disturbed.
    - Use earthy colors like browns and deep greens in your decor.
    - Light incense with grounding scents such as vetiver, cedarwood, or myrrh.
2. **Ground Yourself:**
    - Sit or lie down comfortably.
    - Close your eyes and take deep breaths, inhaling peace and exhaling tension.
    - Visualize roots extending from your body into the Earth, anchoring you firmly.
3. **Visualize the Ankylosaurus:**
    - Imagine standing in a prehistoric landscape.
    - See the Ankylosaurus approaching you, its armor gleaming, exuding strength and protection.
4. **Absorb Its Energy:**
    - As the Ankylosaurus stands beside you, feel its protective energy enveloping you.
    - Visualize its armored plates forming around your body, creating a shield of light that is both flexible and impenetrable.
5. **Set Your Intentions:**
    - Mentally state your intention to build spiritual armor for protection and resilience.
    - Affirmations can include:
        - "I am protected by the armor of the Ankylosaurus."
        - "Negative energies cannot penetrate my shield."

6. **Express Gratitude:**
    - Thank the Ankylosaurus for sharing its strength.
    - Gently return to your conscious awareness, maintaining the feeling of protection.

Rituals for Magickal Fortification
1. Armor-Building Ritual
This ritual is designed to strengthen your spiritual defenses and create a lasting protective barrier.

- **Materials Needed:**
    - A gray or black candle (representing armor and protection)
    - A piece of hematite or black tourmaline
    - A small mirror
    - Salt (preferably sea salt)
- **Steps:**
    - **Create a Sacred Space:**
        - Cleanse your space with sage or incense.
        - Cast a circle of protection if that aligns with your practice.
    - **Set Up Your Altar:**
        - Place the candle at the center.
        - Arrange the stone, mirror, and a bowl of salt around it.
    - **Light the Candle:**
        - As you light it, focus on the flame representing your inner strength.
    - **Invoke the Ankylosaurus:**
        - Say aloud:

"Ankylosaurus, armored knight,
Grant me strength, protect my light.
Build for me a shield so strong,
To guard me as I journey on."

-
    - **Build Your Armor:**
        - Hold the hematite or black tourmaline in your hand.
        - Visualize layers of armor forming around you, starting from your feet and moving upward.
        - See each layer interlocking like the plates of the Ankylosaurus, glowing with protective energy.
    - **Seal the Protection:**
        - Take a pinch of salt and sprinkle it around yourself, forming a protective barrier.
        - Look into the mirror and affirm:

"I am shielded, I am strong,
Protected from all that is wrong."

-
    - **Close the Ritual:**
        - Thank the Ankylosaurus for its guidance.

- Allow the candle to burn down safely or extinguish it if necessary.

2. Foundation-Strengthening Spell

Strengthen the foundation of your magickal practice with this spell, ensuring stability and longevity.

- **Materials Needed:**
  - Four stones representing the four elements (e.g., quartz for air, carnelian for fire, blue lace agate for water, and petrified wood for earth)
  - A square piece of cloth
  - A piece of paper and pen
  - Brown or green ribbon
- **Steps:**
  - **Set Your Intentions:**
    - On the piece of paper, write down the key aspects you wish to strengthen in your practice (e.g., discipline, knowledge, intuition).
  - **Create the Foundation:**
    - Place the four stones at the corners of the cloth, forming a square (symbolizing a strong foundation).
  - **Invoke the Ankylosaurus:**
    - Say:

"Ankylosaurus, steadfast and true,
Help me build a foundation anew.
With Earth and stone, my path secure,
A practice strong and ever pure."

  - **Assemble the Bundle:**
    - Place the paper in the center of the cloth.
    - Gather the corners of the cloth together, enclosing the stones and paper inside.
  - **Tie the Bundle:**
    - Use the ribbon to tie the cloth securely, creating a bundle.
  - **Empower the Bundle:**
    - Hold the bundle to your heart, visualizing it glowing with a warm, grounding light.
    - Affirm:

"My magickal foundation is solid and strong,
Anchored like the Ankylosaurus all along."

  - **Keep the Bundle:**

- Place it on your altar or in a sacred space as a continual reinforcement of your intention.

Incorporating Ankylosaurus Energy into Daily Life

- **Wear Protective Symbols:** Adorn yourself with jewelry or talismans featuring Ankylosaurus imagery or symbols of armor to maintain a constant connection.
- **Visualize Your Armor:** In moments of stress or vulnerability, take a moment to visualize your spiritual armor strengthening and protecting you.
- **Ground Regularly:** Practice grounding exercises, such as walking barefoot on the Earth or meditating with grounding stones, to reinforce your foundation.
- **Set Firm Boundaries:** Be assertive in establishing personal boundaries, both energetically and in your relationships.
- **Affirmations:** Use daily affirmations to reinforce your resilience and protection, such as:
    - "I am fortified by the strength of the Ankylosaurus."
    - "My spiritual armor shields me from all negativity."

Key Lessons from Ankylosaurus Energy

Embracing the Ankylosaurus's energy can profoundly impact your magickal practice and personal growth:

1. **Protection is Proactive:** Building your defenses before challenges arise ensures you are prepared for any situation.
2. **Strength Through Stability:** A solid foundation in your practice allows you to grow and evolve securely.
3. **Resilience is Essential:** Cultivating inner strength helps you navigate obstacles with confidence.
4. **Boundaries Safeguard Energy:** Establishing clear boundaries prevents energy depletion and maintains your well-being.

The Legacy of the Ankylosaurus

The Ankylosaurus stands as a testament to the power of resilience and the effectiveness of a well-fortified defense. Its energy teaches us that protection and strength come not from aggression but from preparation, stability, and an unyielding foundation. By integrating Ankylosaurus magick into your spiritual practice, you create a shield that not only guards against negativity but also supports your growth and evolution.

Let the Ankylosaurus guide you in crafting your spiritual armor, empowering you to face the world with confidence and unwavering strength. As you build upon this unshakable foundation, your magickal practice will flourish, protected and fortified by the enduring legacy of this ancient guardian.

Chapter 10: The Elemental Forces of Dinosaurs

Dinosaurs, as ancient creatures of immense power and diversity, connect deeply with the elemental forces that govern life: **fire, earth, water, and air.** Each element embodies specific energies and qualities, and the dinosaurs that once roamed the Earth can be seen as physical manifestations of these primal forces. By understanding how dinosaurs represent these elements, you can incorporate their energy into your magickal rituals and deepen your connection to the natural world.

In this chapter, we will explore the symbolic relationships between dinosaurs and the four elements, the qualities each element brings to magickal practice, and practical ways to invoke their energies in your rituals.

The Four Elements and Their Energies

The four elements—fire, earth, water, and air—are the building blocks of existence in both the physical and spiritual realms. They are foundational to many magickal practices, each offering unique energies that can be harnessed for transformation, manifestation, and healing.

- **Fire:** Represents passion, courage, and transformation. It is the force of creation and destruction, sparking change and fueling ambition.
- **Earth:** Symbolizes stability, grounding, and abundance. It provides a foundation for growth and sustenance.
- **Water:** Embodies intuition, emotion, and healing. It flows through the subconscious, connecting with dreams and the deep currents of the soul.
- **Air:** Represents intellect, communication, and freedom. It carries ideas, inspiration, and the breath of life itself.

Dinosaurs, as ancient beings that thrived in a world shaped by these elements, offer unique insights into how these forces interact and balance each other.

Dinosaurs and Their Elemental Associations

Each type of dinosaur resonates strongly with one or more elements based on its characteristics, habitat, and behavior. Below are examples of elemental dinosaur archetypes and the lessons they offer:

Fire: The Transformative Energy of Carnivorous Dinosaurs

- **Associated Dinosaurs:**
    - *Tyrannosaurus rex:* The apex predator symbolizes fiery courage, dominance, and the transformative power of destruction.
    - *Allosaurus:* Represents unrelenting drive and the fire of survival.
- **Magickal Lessons:**
    - Embrace passion and courage to pursue your goals.
    - Channel the energy of transformation to overcome obstacles and initiate change.

Earth: The Grounding Strength of Herbivorous Giants

- **Associated Dinosaurs:**
    - *Brontosaurus:* Embodies stability, grounding, and quiet strength.
    - *Ankylosaurus:* Represents resilience and fortification, deeply connected to the Earth.
    - *Stegosaurus:* Symbolizes protection, rootedness, and enduring strength.
- **Magickal Lessons:**
    - Ground yourself to create stability and balance in your life.
    - Build resilience and fortify your foundations to weather challenges.

Water: The Intuitive Flow of Aquatic and Amphibious Dinosaurs

- **Associated Dinosaurs:**
    - *Spinosaurus:* With its aquatic adaptations, it represents emotional depth, intuition, and adaptability.
    - *Ichthyosaurus:* Embodies the healing and life-giving properties of water.
- **Magickal Lessons:**
    - Connect with your intuition and emotional currents to guide your decisions.
    - Use the flow of water energy for healing and emotional release.

Air: The Freedom and Vision of Flying Dinosaurs

- **Associated Dinosaurs:**
    - *Pterodactyl:* Represents freedom, perspective, and the ability to rise above earthly concerns.
    - *Quetzalcoatlus:* Symbolizes ascension, intellect, and spiritual connection.

- **Magickal Lessons:**
    - Gain clarity and insight by adopting a higher perspective.
    - Use air energy to inspire creativity and open channels of communication.

Incorporating Dinosaur Elemental Forces into Your Rituals

To work with the elemental forces of dinosaurs, you can design rituals that invoke the energy of a specific element or balance all four for holistic empowerment. Below are practical rituals for each element, inspired by their dinosaur archetypes.

Fire Ritual: Igniting Courage and Passion

Use this ritual to spark motivation, fuel ambition, or ignite transformative change.

- **Materials Needed:**
    - A red or orange candle
    - A representation of a fiery dinosaur (*e.g., Tyrannosaurus rex figurine or image*)
    - A piece of carnelian or fire opal
- **Steps:**
    - Light the candle and place the dinosaur representation nearby.
    - Hold the carnelian and focus on its warmth, imagining the fiery energy of the *T. rex* flowing into you.
    - Say:

Tyrant king of ancient flame,
Ignite my spirit, bold and untamed.
With fiery strength, I rise anew,
Courage burns, my dreams pursue.

-
    - Visualize a fire igniting within you, fueling your passion and determination.

Earth Ritual: Establishing Stability and Grounding
This ritual helps you anchor yourself in stability and fortify your foundations.

- **Materials Needed:**
    - A green or brown candle
    - A representation of an earth-aligned dinosaur (*e.g., Brontosaurus figurine or image*)
    - A piece of jasper or petrified wood
- **Steps:**
    - Light the candle and place the dinosaur representation in front of you.
    - Hold the jasper or petrified wood and feel its grounding energy.
    - Say:

Gentle giant of strength and grace,
Root me firmly in this sacred space.
With Earth's power, I stand secure,
Resilient, strong, my spirit pure.

-
    - Visualize roots growing from your feet into the Earth, anchoring you in stability and peace.

Water Ritual: Enhancing Intuition and Emotional Healing

Use this ritual to connect with your intuition or release emotional blockages.

- **Materials Needed:**
    - A blue or silver candle
    - A bowl of water
    - A representation of a water-aligned dinosaur (*e.g., Spinosaurus figurine or image*)
    - A piece of aquamarine or moonstone
- **Steps:**
    - Light the candle and place it beside the bowl of water.
    - Hold the aquamarine and focus on the calming flow of water energy.
    - Say:

Spinosaurus of river and sea,
Flow through my soul, set my spirit free.
With water's grace, emotions heal,
Intuition speaks, my truths reveal.

-
    - Dip your fingers in the water and touch your forehead, heart, and hands, symbolizing clarity, love, and action.

Air Ritual: Gaining Clarity and Freedom

Invoke air energy to inspire creativity, clear your mind, or open channels of communication.

- **Materials Needed:**
    - A white or yellow candle
    - A feather
    - A representation of an air-aligned dinosaur (*e.g., Pterodactyl figurine or image*)
    - A piece of clear quartz or citrine
- **Steps:**
    - Light the candle and place the feather and dinosaur representation nearby.
    - Hold the clear quartz and focus on the lightness and clarity of air energy.
    - Say:

Pterodactyl of skies so high,
Lift my spirit, help me fly.
With winds of thought, my mind is clear,
Inspiration flows, my path sincere.

-
    - Visualize yourself soaring through the sky, gaining a higher perspective and freedom from constraints.

Balancing All Four Elements

For holistic empowerment, you can create a ritual that invokes all four elements and their dinosaur archetypes.

Materials Needed:

- Representations of a dinosaur for each element (*e.g., T. rex for fire, Brontosaurus for earth, Spinosaurus for water, and Pterodactyl for air*)
- Candles in red, green, blue, and white
- Stones or symbols corresponding to each element

Steps:

1. Arrange the candles in a circle, placing the representations of the dinosaurs beside them.
2. Light each candle, calling upon the corresponding element and dinosaur energy:
    - **Fire:** "Tyrannosaurus, ignite my passion and courage."
    - **Earth:** "Brontosaurus, ground me in strength and stability."
    - **Water:** "Spinosaurus, flow through my soul with healing and intuition."
    - **Air:** "Pterodactyl, lift me to clarity and inspiration."
3. Stand in the center of the circle and visualize the energies of all four elements merging within you, creating balance and harmony.
4. Close the ritual with gratitude to the dinosaurs and the elemental forces.

Key Lessons from the Elemental Forces of Dinosaurs

1. **Balance is Power:** True strength lies in harmonizing the energies of fire, earth, water, and air.
2. **Diversity in Strength:** Each dinosaur and element offers unique qualities that contribute to your growth.
3. **Connection to Nature:** Working with these forces deepens your relationship with the natural world and its ancient wisdom.

Conclusion

The elemental forces of fire, earth, water, and air are fundamental to life and magick, and dinosaurs, as embodiments of these primal energies, provide a unique lens through which to engage with them. By incorporating the energy of specific dinosaurs into your rituals, you can create powerful connections to the elements, fostering balance, strength, and transformation in your spiritual practice. Let the ancient wisdom of these prehistoric beings guide you as you work with the elemental forces to shape your reality and empower your magick.

Chapter 11: Fossil Magick and Ancestral Energy

Fossils, remnants of prehistoric life preserved in stone, are more than mere artifacts of the Earth's history. They are tangible links to an ancient world, carrying the vibrations of lifeforms that thrived millions of years ago. In magickal practice, fossils serve as powerful tools for connecting with ancestral energy, the spirits of dinosaurs, and the primal forces of the Earth. Their ancient wisdom and transformative power can be harnessed to deepen your rituals, enhance grounding, and amplify your connection to the past.

In this chapter, you will discover how to incorporate fossils into your magickal practice, explore their spiritual significance, and learn rituals to connect with the Earth's ancient history and the energies of dinosaurs.

The Spiritual Significance of Fossils

Fossils are sacred relics that embody a unique combination of earthly and spiritual energies. Their magickal significance lies in their ability to:

1. **Preserve Ancient Energy:** Fossils retain the vibrational imprint of the lifeforms they once were, serving as vessels for prehistoric energy.
2. **Connect to Ancestral Spirits:** By working with fossils, you can tap into the spirits of dinosaurs and other ancient beings, accessing their wisdom and guidance.
3. **Symbolize Transformation:** Fossils are the result of natural transformation, teaching us about the cycles of life, death, and rebirth.
4. **Ground and Protect:** As objects deeply tied to the Earth, fossils provide grounding energy and protection in rituals and meditations.
5. **Act as Magickal Amplifiers:** Their age and unique composition make fossils potent tools for amplifying the energy of your intentions.

Types of Fossils and Their Magickal Uses

Different types of fossils carry specific energies and can be used in magickal work based on their characteristics:

1. Dinosaur Bones

- **Energy:** Resilience, strength, and grounding.
- **Use in Magick:** Enhances physical endurance, fortifies your foundation in life, and connects you to the spirits of dinosaurs.

2. Ammonites

- **Energy:** Transformation, flow, and cycles.
- **Use in Magick:** Ideal for rituals involving change, personal growth, or aligning with natural cycles.

3. Trilobites

- **Energy:** Adaptability, protection, and ancient wisdom.
- **Use in Magick:** Helps you navigate change and offers insight into complex situations.

4. Petrified Wood

- **Energy:** Stability, patience, and grounding.
- **Use in Magick:** Provides a deep connection to the Earth, supports long-term goals, and enhances perseverance.

5. Amber (Fossilized Resin)

- **Energy:** Preservation, healing, and purification.
- **Use in Magick:** Cleanses negative energy, promotes emotional healing, and protects against spiritual harm.

Connecting with the Spirits of Dinosaurs

Fossils are not just physical remnants; they are also spiritual doorways to the energies of the creatures they once were. To connect with the spirits of dinosaurs through fossils, follow these steps:

1. Choose Your Fossil

Select a fossil that resonates with your intention. For example:

- A dinosaur bone for strength and resilience.
- Ammonite for transformation and flow.

2. Cleanse and Consecrate the Fossil

To prepare the fossil for magickal use:

- Cleanse it using smoke (sage or palo santo), moonlight, or saltwater.
- Consecrate it by holding it in your hands and stating your intention for its use.

3. Meditate with the Fossil

Sit in a quiet space, holding the fossil. Close your eyes and visualize the world in which the creature lived. Imagine its spirit awakening and sharing its wisdom with you.

4. Journal or Reflect

After the meditation, write down any insights, feelings, or messages you received.

Fossil Magick Rituals

1. Grounding and Stability Ritual

Use this ritual to connect deeply with the Earth and anchor yourself in stability.

- **Materials Needed:**
    - A piece of petrified wood or dinosaur bone.
    - A green or brown candle.
    - A bowl of soil or Earth.
- **Steps:**
    - Light the candle and place the fossil and bowl of soil in front of you.
    - Hold the fossil and visualize roots extending from your body into the Earth.
    - Say:

Ancient Earth, my foundation strong,
Through fossil's power, I belong.
Ground my spirit, steady my way,
Keep me centered, come what may.

-
    - Place the fossil in the soil as a symbolic act of grounding.
    - Allow the candle to burn down safely.

2. Ritual for Ancestral Wisdom

Call upon the spirits of dinosaurs to gain insight and guidance in your life.

- **Materials Needed:**
  - A dinosaur fossil (bone or ammonite preferred).
  - A purple or silver candle.
  - Incense (frankincense or sandalwood).
- **Steps:**
  - Light the candle and incense, creating a sacred space.
  - Hold the fossil in your hands and close your eyes.
  - Say:

Spirits of the ancient past,
Through this fossil, wisdom cast.
Guide my steps, my path reveal,
Through your power, truths unseal.

  - Sit in meditation, allowing any images, thoughts, or sensations to arise.
  - Thank the spirits and extinguish the candle.

3. Protection Spell with Fossil Energy

Create a protective barrier using the fortifying energy of fossils.

- **Materials Needed:**
  - A piece of amber or trilobite fossil.
  - A black candle.
  - A circle of salt.
- **Steps:**
  - Place the candle and fossil at the center of the circle of salt.
  - Light the candle and focus on the fossil's energy forming a protective shield around you.
  - Say:

Fossil of ages, guard me well,
With ancient power, form a shell.
No harm may enter, no ill may stay,
Protected I am, night and day.

  - Leave the fossil in the circle of salt overnight to amplify its protective energy.

Incorporating Fossils into Daily Magick

- **Wear Fossil Jewelry:** Carry the energy of fossils with you by wearing them as pendants, rings, or bracelets.
- **Place Fossils on Your Altar:** Use fossils to anchor your sacred space and connect it to the Earth's ancient energy.
- **Meditate Daily with Fossils:** Strengthen your connection to prehistoric wisdom by holding a fossil during meditation.
- **Use Fossils in Divination:** Place a fossil on your tarot or rune spread to gain insight grounded in ancestral energy.

Key Lessons from Fossil Magick

1. **Ancient Energy Lives On:** Fossils remind us that energy is eternal and transformation is a natural part of existence.
2. **Grounding Is Essential:** Working with fossils helps you stay rooted and balanced, providing stability in your spiritual practice.
3. **Wisdom Is Timeless:** The spirits of dinosaurs and ancient creatures offer guidance that transcends time and space.
4. **Transformation Is Power:** Fossils, as symbols of change, inspire you to embrace transformation in your life and magick.

Conclusion

Fossils are extraordinary tools in magick, bridging the gap between the ancient past and the present. By incorporating them into your spiritual practice, you gain access to the wisdom of the Earth's earliest inhabitants, the resilience of their energy, and the grounding stability of their legacy. Whether used for protection, grounding, or ancestral connection, fossils enrich your rituals with their profound, timeless power.

Let the fossils guide you, teaching you the lessons of endurance, transformation, and the deep currents of Earth's magickal history. Through them, you connect not only to the spirits of dinosaurs but also to the infinite cycles of life and the enduring strength of the Earth itself.

Chapter 12: Dino Bones and Magickal Artifacts

Dinosaur bones, whether real fossils or symbolic representations, are powerful magickal artifacts that embody the timeless energy of the Earth and its ancient creatures. These sacred objects serve as conduits to prehistoric wisdom, resilience, and transformative power. When incorporated into rituals and ceremonies, dinosaur bones amplify your magickal intentions, protect your space, and connect you to the primal forces of nature.

In this chapter, we will explore the significance of dinosaur bones in magick, how to ethically source and consecrate them, and detailed rituals and ceremonies for their use.

The Symbolism of Dinosaur Bones

Dinosaur bones are potent symbols in magick due to their unique attributes:

1. **Eternal Memory:** These remnants of prehistoric life hold the Earth's ancient history and energy, serving as links to a time of immense power and transformation.
2. **Resilience and Strength:** Bones are the framework of life, representing structure, endurance, and unyielding strength.
3. **Transformation and Rebirth:** Fossilized bones symbolize the natural cycles of death and rebirth, teaching us to embrace change.
4. **Spiritual Anchors:** They provide a grounded connection to the Earth while facilitating spiritual exploration and empowerment.

Sourcing and Selecting Dinosaur Bones

If you wish to incorporate dinosaur bones into your magickal practice, it's essential to approach the process with respect and ethical consideration.

1. Sourcing Real Fossils

- **Ethical Acquisition:** Purchase from reputable dealers or museums that provide certification of authenticity and adhere to ethical practices.
- **Legal Considerations:** Ensure that acquiring and owning fossils is legal in your region.

2. Using Symbolic Bones

- **Alternative Materials:** Replica dinosaur bones, carved stones, or sculpted representations can serve as substitutes while still carrying symbolic power.
- **Personal Connection:** Choose materials that resonate with you, such as clay models or wooden carvings, and imbue them with intention through consecration.

3. Creating Your Own Artifact

- **Crafting Symbols:** Create your own symbolic dinosaur bones from natural materials like clay, bone-shaped stones, or wood.
- **Personalization:** Add carvings, sigils, or colors that align with your magickal intentions.

Consecrating Dinosaur Bones as Sacred Artifacts

Before using dinosaur bones in rituals, they must be cleansed and consecrated to align them with your energy and magickal purpose.

1. Cleansing the Bones

- **Smoke Cleansing:** Use sage, palo santo, or incense to cleanse the bones of any residual energy. Pass them through the smoke while stating your intention.
- **Moonlight or Sunlight:** Place the bones under the moonlight for spiritual cleansing or in sunlight for energizing and activating.
- **Salt Purification:** Bury the bones in a bowl of sea salt for 24 hours to neutralize any negative energy.

2. Consecration Ritual

- **Materials Needed:**
  - A white candle (for purity)
  - A bowl of water (for emotional balance)
  - A bowl of soil (for grounding)
  - Incense (for air energy)
- **Steps:**
  - Light the candle and incense, creating a sacred space.
  - Place the bones in the center of your altar or workspace.
  - Say:

Bones of ancient Earth, I call to thee,
Vessel of wisdom, power, and eternity.
Cleanse and bless, aligned with my will,
A sacred tool, magickal and still.

-
  - Pass the bones through the smoke, sprinkle them with water, and place them on the soil, symbolizing their alignment with the elements.
  - Visualize a glowing light infusing the bones, charging them with energy and purpose.

Rituals and Ceremonies with Dinosaur Bones

Dinosaur bones can be used in a variety of rituals, from protection spells to ancestral connection ceremonies. Below are detailed examples:

1. Protection Ritual with Dinosaur Bones

This ritual creates a powerful protective barrier using the resilience of dinosaur bones.

- **Materials Needed:**
  - A dinosaur bone or symbolic artifact
  - A black candle (for protection)
  - A circle of salt
- **Steps:**
  - Light the black candle and place the dinosaur bone in the center of the circle of salt.
  - Visualize the bone radiating a protective shield around you or your space.
  - Say:

Guardian of Earth from ages past,
Protect me now, a spell I cast.
With ancient strength, my shield is made,
No harm shall pass, no ill invade.

-
  - Let the candle burn while focusing on the protective energy surrounding you.

2. Ritual for Connecting with Prehistoric Wisdom
Use this ritual to access the ancient knowledge stored within dinosaur bones.

- **Materials Needed:**
    - A dinosaur bone or replica
    - A purple or silver candle
    - A piece of amethyst
- **Steps:**
    - Light the candle and hold the bone in your hands.
    - Close your eyes and visualize the prehistoric world. Imagine yourself walking among dinosaurs, sensing their energy.
    - Say:

Keeper of wisdom, so ancient and deep,
Share your knowledge, awake from sleep.
Guide my spirit, teach me your way,
Wisdom of eons, in my soul, stay.

-
    - Meditate with the bone, allowing messages or insights to flow into your mind.

3. Ancestor Connection Ceremony
This ceremony honors the spirits of dinosaurs and aligns you with the Earth's ancient lineage.

- **Materials Needed:**
    - A set of dinosaur bones (real or symbolic)
    - A green candle (for Earth energy)
    - A bowl of soil or Earth
- **Steps:**
    - Arrange the bones around the green candle and the bowl of soil.
    - Light the candle and place your hands over the soil.
    - Say:

Ancestors of Earth, guardians of time,
I call upon your spirit, ancient and prime.
Through these bones, our lineage flows,
In your wisdom, my path grows.

-
    - Spend time reflecting or meditating, allowing the connection to deepen.

Incorporating Dinosaur Bones into Daily Magick

- **Place Bones on Your Altar:** Use dinosaur bones as focal points for grounding energy in your sacred space.
- **Carry Them as Talismans:** Keep small dinosaur bone fragments or replicas in your pocket or pouch for ongoing protection and strength.
- **Meditate with Them Regularly:** Hold a dinosaur bone during meditation to stay connected to its ancient energy.
- **Use Them in Divination:** Place a dinosaur bone on your tarot or rune spread to draw upon its wisdom for guidance.

Key Lessons from Dinosaur Bones

1. **Strength in Stillness:** Like bones preserved over millions of years, resilience is found in remaining steadfast and grounded.
2. **Transformation is Eternal:** Fossilized bones remind us of the power of change and the cycles of life and rebirth.
3. **Connection to the Ancient Past:** Working with dinosaur bones deepens your bond with the Earth's history and its primal energies.
4. **Tools of Protection:** Bones serve as powerful guardians, shielding you from negativity and external harm.

Conclusion

Dinosaur bones are extraordinary magickal artifacts that carry the energy of resilience, protection, and ancient wisdom. Whether real fossils or symbolic representations, these sacred tools connect you to the Earth's prehistoric past and empower your rituals with their timeless strength.

By incorporating dinosaur bones into your practice, you can create a magickal foundation rooted in the power of nature's oldest guardians. Let the bones guide you, protect you, and inspire you to embrace the cycles of transformation and the enduring legacy of life on Earth.

Chapter 13: The Lost Land: Tapping into Prehistoric Earth Energy

The Mesozoic Era, often referred to as the "Age of Dinosaurs," was a time when the Earth pulsed with primal energy, its landscapes untouched by modern civilizations. Towering forests, volcanic plains, and shifting continents created an ecosystem where dinosaurs thrived for millions of years. This era holds a powerful resonance for those who wish to connect with the Earth's raw, untainted energy.

By journeying into the energetic landscapes of the Mesozoic Era, you can tap into the primal forces of life, growth, and resilience. This chapter will guide you through understanding prehistoric Earth energy, how to access it, and incorporating it into your magickal practices for empowerment, grounding, and transformation.

The Energy of the Mesozoic Era

The Mesozoic Era spanned over 180 million years and comprised three distinct periods: the Triassic, Jurassic, and Cretaceous. Each period contributed unique energetic qualities to the Earth's spiritual tapestry:

1. **Triassic Period (251–201 million years ago):**
    - Symbolizes beginnings, adaptation, and survival.
    - The first dinosaurs emerged, representing new cycles and potential.
2. **Jurassic Period (201–145 million years ago):**
    - Embodies growth, abundance, and the flourishing of life.
    - Lush forests and diverse ecosystems reflect creativity and expansion.
3. **Cretaceous Period (145–66 million years ago):**
    - Represents transformation, resilience, and cycles of renewal.
    - The evolution of advanced dinosaurs and their eventual extinction mirrors the balance of creation and destruction.

The energy of these periods holds lessons in adaptability, abundance, and transformation that can enhance your spiritual growth.

Connecting with Prehistoric Earth Energy

To tap into the Earth's Mesozoic energy, you must develop a deep connection to the primal forces that shaped the planet. This involves immersing yourself in the Earth's ancient rhythms, both physically and spiritually.

1. Grounding in Nature

- Spend time in forests, deserts, or other natural environments to attune yourself to the Earth's energy.
- Walk barefoot to connect physically with the ground and imagine the landscapes of the Mesozoic beneath your feet.

2. Meditating with Fossils and Stones

- Hold fossils, petrified wood, or volcanic stones during meditation to connect with the Earth's prehistoric vibrations.
- Visualize the landscapes of the Mesozoic—volcanic plains, towering trees, and sprawling lakes—and imagine their energy flowing into you.

3. Working with Dinosaurs as Totems

- Choose a dinosaur that resonates with your goals or intentions (e.g., T. rex for courage, Brontosaurus for grounding).
- Meditate on its energy, imagining how it thrived in its environment and what lessons it can teach you about resilience and adaptation.

Prehistoric Energy Rituals
1. Ritual of Mesozoic Grounding
This ritual helps you anchor yourself in the primal energy of the Earth, enhancing stability and resilience.

- **Materials Needed:**
  - A piece of petrified wood or volcanic rock.
  - A green or brown candle.
  - A bowl of soil.
- **Steps:**
  - Light the candle and place the petrified wood or rock in the bowl of soil.
  - Sit comfortably and hold the bowl in your hands.
  - Close your eyes and visualize the Mesozoic landscape—lush forests, volcanic eruptions, and thriving dinosaurs.
  - Say:

Earth of ages, ancient and wise,
Root me deeply, where your power lies.
Through time's expanse, your strength remains,
Ground me now, as your wisdom sustains.

-
  - Feel the energy of the Earth anchoring you and filling you with stability.

2. Journey to the Lost Land

This guided meditation takes you on a spiritual journey to the Mesozoic Era to connect with its primal energy.

1. **Preparation:**
    - Use a fossil or stone as a focus object.
    - Light incense such as cedar or frankincense to evoke Earth energy.
2. **Meditation Steps:**
    - Sit or lie down in a comfortable position, holding your focus object.
    - Close your eyes and take deep breaths, visualizing yourself traveling back in time.
    - Picture the Earth transforming around you—modern landscapes fading into prehistoric forests, mountains, and plains.
    - Imagine yourself standing in the Mesozoic Era, surrounded by dinosaurs and ancient plant life.
    - Feel the vibrations of the Earth beneath your feet and the primal energy of the ecosystem flowing through you.
3. **Integration:**
    - After your journey, slowly return to the present moment, bringing the energy of the Mesozoic with you.
    - Journal your experiences and any messages or insights you received.

3. Ritual for Renewal and Transformation

This ritual harnesses the transformative energy of the Cretaceous Period to help you embrace change and renewal.

- **Materials Needed:**
    - A piece of amber (fossilized resin) or clear quartz.
    - A yellow or gold candle.
    - A small piece of paper and pen.
- **Steps:**
    - Write down an aspect of your life you wish to transform or renew on the paper.
    - Light the candle and hold the amber or quartz in your hands.
    - Visualize the landscapes of the Cretaceous Period, imagining the cycle of life and transformation.
    - Say:

From Earth's ancient cycles, I draw my power,
Transformation blooms, like life's first flower.
What no longer serves, I leave behind,
Renewal and strength now fill my mind.

-
    - Burn the paper in the candle flame, symbolizing the release of the old and the embrace of the new.

Incorporating Prehistoric Earth Energy in Daily Life

- **Use Prehistoric Stones:** Carry fossils, petrified wood, or volcanic rocks to maintain a connection to Mesozoic energy throughout the day.
- **Visualize Mesozoic Landscapes:** During moments of stress or uncertainty, imagine yourself in the calm strength of a prehistoric forest or the vibrant life of a dinosaur plain.
- **Practice Elemental Magick:** Work with the elements of fire, earth, water, and air to recreate the dynamic forces of the Mesozoic Era.
- **Honor the Lost Land:** Create an altar dedicated to prehistoric Earth, including fossils, bones, and representations of dinosaurs, as a focal point for your spiritual practice.

Lessons from the Lost Land

The energetic landscapes of the Mesozoic Era offer profound lessons for personal and spiritual growth:

1. **Adaptation is Key:** The evolution of dinosaurs teaches us to embrace change and adapt to shifting circumstances.
2. **Life is Cyclical:** The rise and fall of prehistoric life reminds us of the natural cycles of creation, destruction, and renewal.
3. **Balance Strength and Grace:** Dinosaurs thrived by balancing their physical strength with adaptability, a lesson in harmonizing power with flexibility.
4. **Primal Energy Endures:** The energy of the Earth's ancient past continues to flow, offering grounding and empowerment to those who seek it.

Conclusion

Tapping into the primal Earth energy of the Mesozoic Era allows you to access a timeless reservoir of strength, resilience, and transformation. By journeying to the Lost Land through rituals, meditations, and magickal practices, you connect with the ancient wisdom of the Earth and its creatures, empowering your spiritual path.

Let the landscapes of the Mesozoic Era inspire and guide you, as you draw on the power of prehistoric Earth to ground yourself, embrace transformation, and align with the enduring cycles of nature. Through this connection, the Lost Land becomes not just a relic of the past, but a living force in your magickal practice and spiritual journey.

Chapter 14: Creating a Dinosaur Altar

An altar is a sacred space that acts as a focal point for your energy, intentions, and rituals. A **dinosaur-themed altar** can serve as a powerful tool to connect with the ancient energies of these prehistoric beings, drawing on their strength, wisdom, and primal force. By curating an altar dedicated to dinosaurs, you create a bridge between the modern world and the Mesozoic Era, focusing your spiritual practice on grounding, protection, transformation, and resilience.

In this chapter, you'll learn how to design, set up, and use a dinosaur altar to amplify your connection to these ancient creatures, enhance your rituals, and deepen your spiritual practice.

The Purpose of a Dinosaur Altar

A dinosaur altar serves multiple purposes in your magickal and spiritual practice:

1. **Focal Point for Rituals:** Acts as a central space for performing rituals, meditations, and spellwork involving dinosaur energy.
2. **Connection to Ancient Energy:** Provides a dedicated place to commune with the spirits of dinosaurs and the Earth's prehistoric energy.
3. **Amplification of Intentions:** Focuses and enhances the energy of your magickal intentions.
4. **Symbol of Resilience and Power:** Serves as a daily reminder of the strength, adaptability, and wisdom of dinosaurs.

Choosing the Location for Your Altar

The location of your altar is an important consideration, as it affects the energy and accessibility of the space:

1. **Sacred Space:** Select a quiet, undisturbed area where you can focus and feel connected to the Earth.
2. **Natural Setting:** If possible, place your altar near a window with natural light, or even outdoors, to align with the natural elements dinosaurs thrived in.
3. **Accessibility:** Ensure the altar is easily accessible for daily use, rituals, or meditation.
4. **Energetic Flow:** Position your altar in a place that feels energetically harmonious and grounded.

Designing Your Dinosaur Altar
1. Foundation and Structure
The foundation of your altar should reflect the themes of strength, grounding, and resilience:

- Use a sturdy table, shelf, or flat surface.
- Consider natural materials like wood or stone for an earthy feel.

2. Dinosaur Representations
Incorporate symbolic or physical representations of dinosaurs:

- **Figurines or Statues:** Choose figurines that represent specific dinosaurs you wish to connect with, such as a Tyrannosaurus rex for courage or a Stegosaurus for protection.
- **Artwork:** Display images or illustrations of dinosaurs to evoke their energy visually.
- **Fossils or Replicas:** Real or symbolic fossils add a tangible connection to the Earth's ancient history.

3. Elemental Correspondences
Balance your altar with representations of the four elements, honoring the primal forces that shaped the Mesozoic Era:

- **Fire:** A red or orange candle to symbolize transformation and courage.
- **Earth:** Fossils, stones (like petrified wood or jasper), or soil for grounding energy.
- **Water:** A small bowl of water to represent adaptability and emotional flow.
- **Air:** Feathers or incense to evoke freedom, intellect, and higher consciousness.

4. Colors and Decor
Use colors that align with dinosaur energy and the natural world:

- **Green and Brown:** Represent the Earth, grounding, and stability.
- **Yellow and Red:** Symbolize fire, passion, and courage.
- **Blue and Silver:** Reflect water, intuition, and the sky.

Decorate with items such as leaves, plants, or prehistoric-inspired symbols to enhance the connection to nature and the Mesozoic environment.

Essential Items for Your Dinosaur Altar

1. **Candles:** Choose colors based on your intentions and the dinosaur archetypes you're working with.
2. **Crystals and Stones:**
    - Petrified wood: Stability and grounding.
    - Ammonite: Transformation and cycles.
    - Amber: Preservation and healing.
    - Obsidian: Protection and resilience.
3. **Fossils or Fossil Replicas:** Dinosaur bones, ammonites, or trilobites to connect with ancient energy.
4. **Altar Cloth:** Use an earthy-toned or dinosaur-patterned cloth to define the space.
5. **Offerings:** Small items like herbs, flowers, or symbolic food offerings to honor the spirits of dinosaurs.
6. **Sacred Tools:** Include tools like a wand, athame, or bowl for use in rituals and ceremonies.

Setting Up Your Dinosaur Altar

Follow these steps to create a meaningful and energetically aligned dinosaur altar:

1. **Cleanse the Space:** Before setting up, cleanse the area with smoke, sound, or a saltwater spray to remove stagnant energy.
2. **Arrange the Foundation:** Place your altar cloth, followed by the main structural items like candles, fossils, or figurines.
3. **Add Representations:** Arrange the dinosaur representations and elemental symbols according to your intuitive or magickal preferences.
4. **Place Tools and Offerings:** Include sacred tools and offerings, arranging them in a way that feels harmonious and balanced.
5. **Dedicate the Altar:** Once the setup is complete, dedicate the altar by lighting the candles and stating your intention. For example:

I dedicate this altar to the wisdom and power of the ancient Earth,
To the spirits of dinosaurs who thrived in strength and resilience.
May this sacred space connect me to their energy,
Guiding and empowering my journey.

Using Your Dinosaur Altar

Your dinosaur altar is a versatile space that can be used for a variety of spiritual and magickal purposes:

1. Daily Meditation

- Sit before your altar and focus on the energy of the dinosaurs represented there.
- Hold a fossil or stone and visualize yourself connecting with their primal power.

2. Rituals and Spellwork

- Perform rituals and spells that align with dinosaur energy, such as protection spells (Stegosaurus), courage invocations (T. rex), or grounding practices (Brontosaurus).
- Use the altar as a focal point to amplify your intentions.

3. Offerings and Gratitude

- Place offerings on the altar to honor the spirits of dinosaurs and the Earth. Examples include herbs, stones, or symbolic food items.
- Regularly express gratitude for the guidance and energy you receive.

4. Seasonal Adaptations

- Update your altar with items that reflect seasonal changes, such as flowers in spring, leaves in autumn, or stones associated with winter.
- Align your altar with the cycles of the Earth to enhance its resonance.

Cleansing and Maintaining Your Dinosaur Altar

To keep the energy of your altar vibrant and aligned, cleanse and refresh it regularly:

1. **Cleansing Rituals:** Use smoke (sage, palo santo, or incense), sound (bells or singing bowls), or moonlight to clear stagnant energy.
2. **Physical Cleaning:** Dust and clean the items and altar space to maintain its physical and energetic purity.
3. **Recharging Items:** Periodically recharge fossils, crystals, and tools by placing them under the sun, moon, or in a bowl of salt.
4. **Refreshing Decor:** Update offerings, candles, or decorations to reflect new intentions or seasons.

Key Lessons from Creating a Dinosaur Altar

1. **Focus and Intention:** An altar is a powerful focal point for your energy, helping you align your intentions with the wisdom and strength of dinosaurs.
2. **Connection to Ancient Power:** By dedicating a space to prehistoric energy, you forge a deeper connection to the Earth's history and primal forces.
3. **Adaptability and Growth:** Regularly updating and maintaining your altar reflects the dynamic cycles of nature and the adaptability of dinosaurs.
4. **Sacred Space:** Your altar is a personal sanctuary where you can reflect, recharge, and perform magickal workings.

Conclusion

Creating a dinosaur-themed altar is a transformative way to connect with the energy of these ancient beings and the Earth's primal power. By designing a space that resonates with your intentions and the qualities of specific dinosaurs, you create a sacred tool for grounding, protection, and spiritual growth.

As you use your dinosaur altar in daily practice, rituals, and meditations, you will deepen your connection to prehistoric energy, harnessing the resilience and wisdom of the creatures that once roamed the Earth. Let your altar be a place of inspiration, empowerment, and transformation as you walk your spiritual path with the guidance of these ancient guardians.

Chapter 15: Dinosaur-Inspired Sigils and Symbols

Sigils and symbols are powerful tools in magick, allowing practitioners to focus and amplify their intentions through visual representation. By drawing inspiration from the forms and energies of dinosaurs, you can create unique sigils and glyphs imbued with the primal power, resilience, and wisdom of these ancient creatures. These symbols not only enhance your magickal practice but also serve as a visual connection to the Earth's prehistoric past.

In this chapter, you'll learn the fundamentals of sigil creation, how to draw from dinosaur archetypes for inspiration, and practical ways to incorporate dinosaur-inspired sigils and symbols into your rituals and spiritual practice.

The Power of Sigils and Symbols

Sigils are crafted symbols that represent specific intentions, often created through a combination of letters, shapes, and abstract designs. When inspired by dinosaurs, these sigils tap into the ancient energy of these creatures, combining their symbolic meanings with your personal goals.

The Benefits of Using Sigils

- **Amplify Intentions:** Sigils focus your magickal energy on a specific goal, acting as a visual and energetic anchor.
- **Enhance Connection:** Dinosaur-inspired symbols deepen your connection to prehistoric energy and Earth's ancient history.
- **Customizable:** Sigils can be personalized to reflect your unique intentions and align with specific dinosaur archetypes.

Drawing Inspiration from Dinosaurs

The forms, behaviors, and symbolic meanings of dinosaurs provide endless inspiration for creating sigils and symbols. Below are some examples of dinosaur archetypes and their corresponding themes:

1. Tyrannosaurus Rex

- **Themes:** Strength, courage, dominance.
- **Inspiration:** Sharp angles, claw-like shapes, and powerful strokes to represent its ferocity and leadership.

2. Stegosaurus

- **Themes:** Protection, resilience, boundaries.
- **Inspiration:** Plate-like designs, spiked motifs, and interlocking shapes to symbolize its defensive armor.

3. Brontosaurus

- **Themes:** Grounding, stability, patience.
- **Inspiration:** Curving lines, arches, and sturdy forms that reflect its massive yet peaceful presence.

4. Pterodactyl

- **Themes:** Freedom, perspective, spiritual ascension.
- **Inspiration:** Wing-like shapes, open designs, and airy patterns to evoke flight and clarity.

5. Velociraptor

- **Themes:** Agility, intellect, adaptability.
- **Inspiration:** Sleek lines, swift strokes, and dynamic designs to capture its speed and cleverness.

Creating Dinosaur-Inspired Sigils

Follow these steps to create a sigil inspired by dinosaur energy:

1. Define Your Intention

Clearly state your goal or intention. For example:

- "I want to be fearless in challenging situations." (T. rex energy)
- "I seek emotional protection and stability." (Stegosaurus energy)

2. Choose a Dinosaur Archetype

Select the dinosaur that best aligns with your intention. Research its characteristics, behaviors, and symbolic meanings to guide your design.

3. Break Down the Intention into Keywords

Identify the core words of your intention. For example:

- Fearless, courage, strength (T. rex)
- Protection, boundaries, stability (Stegosaurus)

4. Simplify the Keywords

Reduce the words to their essential letters. For example:

- "Courage" becomes C-R-G.
- "Protection" becomes P-R-T-C-N.

5. Combine Letters and Shapes

Use the letters as a foundation for your sigil, combining and overlapping them to create a unique design. Incorporate dinosaur-inspired elements such as claws, spikes, wings, or tails to enhance the symbolism.

6. Refine the Design

Streamline your sigil into a cohesive, aesthetically pleasing symbol. Focus on simplicity and balance while maintaining its energetic alignment with your intention.

7. Activate the Sigil

Infuse your sigil with energy by focusing on your intention while drawing, carving, or visualizing it. Methods of activation include:

- Burning: Draw the sigil on paper and burn it while meditating on your goal.
- Charging: Place the sigil under moonlight, sunlight, or on a crystal.
- Visualization: Meditate on the sigil, imagining it glowing with energy.

Examples of Dinosaur-Inspired Sigils
1. Sigil for Courage (T. rex Energy)

- Sharp, angular lines representing claws and teeth.
- A central triangle symbolizing power and dominance.
- Enclosed in a circle to represent focus and containment.

2. Sigil for Protection (Stegosaurus Energy)

- A row of spiked shapes resembling the plates of a Stegosaurus.
- Interlocking patterns to symbolize strong boundaries.
- A shield-like outer frame for added defensive energy.

3. Sigil for Grounding (Brontosaurus Energy)

- Curving lines and arches to evoke stability and rootedness.
- Heavy, solid strokes to reflect the Brontosaurus's weight and presence.
- A spiral at the base to symbolize connection to Earth's energy.

Using Dinosaur-Inspired Sigils

Once your sigil is created and activated, there are many ways to incorporate it into your magickal practice:

1. In Rituals and Spells

- Draw or carve the sigil on candles, stones, or other ritual tools.
- Include it in spellwork by visualizing it glowing with energy as you focus on your intention.

2. As Talismans

- Create wearable sigils by engraving them onto jewelry, amulets, or pendants.
- Carry a small stone or object with the sigil drawn on it for ongoing energy.

3. On Your Altar

- Place the sigil on your dinosaur-themed altar as a focal point for meditations or rituals.
- Combine it with fossils, crystals, and other items to amplify its energy.

4. In Daily Life

- Draw the sigil in a discreet place (e.g., on your skin, a notebook, or a water bottle) to carry its energy throughout the day.
- Use it as a meditative symbol, focusing on it during moments of reflection or stress.

Ritual for Empowering a Dinosaur-Inspired Sigil

This ritual enhances the energy of your sigil, aligning it with the ancient power of dinosaurs.

Materials Needed:

- A completed dinosaur-inspired sigil.
- A fossil or symbolic dinosaur representation.
- A candle in a color corresponding to your intention (e.g., red for courage, green for grounding).
- A small bowl of salt or Earth.

Steps:

1. **Cleanse the Space:** Use smoke, sound, or saltwater to cleanse your ritual space.
2. **Light the Candle:** Place the sigil and fossil in front of the candle.
3. **Focus on Your Intention:** Hold the sigil and visualize your goal clearly in your mind.
4. **Invoke Dinosaur Energy:**

Say:
Spirits of ancient Earth, hear my call,
Through this sigil, may my intentions enthrall.
With primal power, let my goal take flight,
Infuse this symbol with your strength and might.

1. **Charge the Sigil:** Pass the sigil over the flame, fossil, and bowl of salt, symbolizing its activation through fire, Earth, and ancient energy.
2. **Conclude:** Place the sigil on your altar or carry it with you, knowing it is charged and aligned with your intention.

Key Lessons from Dinosaur-Inspired Sigils

1. **Creativity in Connection:** Drawing from dinosaur forms allows you to creatively link with their energies, making your magick more personal and effective.
2. **Focus and Intention:** Sigils sharpen your focus, allowing you to channel your energy toward a specific goal with clarity.
3. **Ancient Power in Modern Practice:** Incorporating prehistoric themes bridges the ancient and modern worlds, enriching your spiritual practice with timeless strength.
4. **Symbolism Enhances Energy:** By embedding dinosaur archetypes into your sigils, you amplify their resonance and align them with your magickal intentions.

Conclusion

Dinosaur-inspired sigils and symbols offer a unique and powerful way to channel the ancient energy of these magnificent creatures into your magickal practice. By combining the visual language of sigils with the symbolic strength of dinosaurs, you create tools that are not only deeply personal but also profoundly effective.

As you incorporate these symbols into your rituals, altars, and daily life, you will find that they enhance your connection to prehistoric power, focus your intentions, and empower your magickal journey. Let your sigils become living expressions of your will, guided by the resilience and wisdom of the ancient Earth.

Chapter 16: Jurassic Lunar Magick

The moon has been a source of mystical power for millennia, influencing tides, emotions, and cycles of life. By combining lunar energy with the primal forces of dinosaurs, you can create a unique and potent practice known as **Jurassic Lunar Magick.** This practice aligns the symbolism of dinosaurs with the moon's phases, allowing you to enhance your rituals, spells, and manifestations through a prehistoric lens.

In this chapter, you will learn the principles of Jurassic Lunar Magick, how to harness the energy of the moon's phases, and how to incorporate dinosaur archetypes into your lunar rituals for maximum magickal impact.

The Power of the Moon in Magick

The moon is deeply tied to the cycles of nature and the rhythms of life. Each lunar phase carries distinct energies that can be harnessed for specific purposes:

1. **New Moon:** A time of beginnings, setting intentions, and planting seeds for growth.
2. **Waxing Crescent:** Energy builds as intentions take form; a period for focus and action.
3. **First Quarter:** Challenges arise, calling for courage and determination to move forward.
4. **Waxing Gibbous:** Refine your intentions and prepare for fruition; a time for clarity and persistence.
5. **Full Moon:** Peak energy for manifestation, celebration, and power.
6. **Waning Gibbous:** Gratitude and release of excess energy; a time for reflection.
7. **Last Quarter:** Let go of what no longer serves; focus on cleansing and transformation.
8. **Waning Crescent:** Rest, introspection, and preparation for the next cycle.

Dinosaur Archetypes and Lunar Energy

Each dinosaur archetype aligns with specific lunar phases and energies, offering a prehistoric lens through which to channel lunar power:

1. **Tyrannosaurus Rex (New Moon & First Quarter):** Symbolizes courage, leadership, and initiating bold actions.
2. **Stegosaurus (Full Moon):** Represents protection, stability, and celebrating accomplishments.
3. **Brontosaurus (Waning Crescent):** Embodies grounding, patience, and reflection during times of rest.
4. **Pterodactyl (Waxing Gibbous & Full Moon):** Aligns with clarity, perspective, and manifesting dreams.
5. **Velociraptor (Waxing Crescent & First Quarter):** Mirrors agility, adaptability, and determination to overcome obstacles.

Creating Jurassic Lunar Rituals

To incorporate Jurassic Lunar Magick into your practice, design rituals that align lunar phases with dinosaur archetypes. Here are steps to guide you:

1. New Moon: Planting Seeds of Intention

- **Dinosaur Archetype:** *Tyrannosaurus Rex* for bold beginnings.
- **Purpose:** Set intentions, initiate new projects, and tap into primal courage.
- **Ritual Steps:**
    1. Light a black or silver candle to represent the darkness of the New Moon and potential for growth.
    2. Place a T. rex figurine or image on your altar as a symbol of bold action.
    3. Write down your intentions for the lunar cycle.
    4. Say:

Tyrant king of ancient might,
Guide my steps, my path ignite.
In this darkness, seeds I sow,
With your courage, dreams will grow.

- 1. Burn your written intentions, visualizing their energy being planted into the universe.

2. Waxing Crescent: Building Momentum

- **Dinosaur Archetype:** *Velociraptor* for focus and determination.
- **Purpose:** Take action on your intentions and build energy toward your goals.
- **Ritual Steps:**
    1. Use a red or orange candle to symbolize rising energy and action.
    2. Hold a small dinosaur claw or sharp stone (symbolic of Velociraptor's precision) as you focus on your goals.
    3. Visualize yourself taking swift, confident steps toward your objectives.
    4. Say:

Swift and sharp, with cunning I move,
Each step forward, my skills improve.
Velociraptor, lend me your speed,
To reach my goals and plant the seed.

3. Full Moon: Manifestation and Celebration

- **Dinosaur Archetype:** *Stegosaurus* for stability and protection; *Pterodactyl* for perspective.
- **Purpose:** Celebrate achievements, amplify power, and protect what you've built.
- **Ritual Steps:**
    1. Arrange your altar with a white or gold candle, fossils, and a Stegosaurus or Pterodactyl representation.
    2. Reflect on what you've accomplished so far in the lunar cycle.
    3. Say:

Full Moon bright, your power I call,
Strength and wisdom, guiding us all.
Stegosaurus, protect what's mine,
Pterodactyl, lift me to heights divine.

-
    1. Meditate under the moonlight, absorbing its energy into your spirit.

4. Waning Crescent: Rest and Reflection

- **Dinosaur Archetype:** *Brontosaurus* for grounding and introspection.
- **Purpose:** Let go of negativity, recharge, and prepare for the next cycle.
- **Ritual Steps:**
    1. Use a green or brown candle to represent grounding energy.
    2. Hold a piece of petrified wood or another Earth-related fossil as you reflect on the past month.
    3. Write down anything you wish to release and bury the paper in soil or sand.
    4. Say:

Gentle giant of Earth and time,
Help me rest, release, and climb.
With patience vast and strength profound,
My soul renews, my spirit is sound.

Enhancing Jurassic Lunar Magick
1. Moonlit Fossil Charging

- Place fossils or dinosaur-inspired tools under the moonlight to absorb its energy.
- Use these charged items in your rituals for added power.

2. Altar Adaptations

- Update your dinosaur altar to reflect the current lunar phase, adding candles, colors, or fossils that align with its energy.

3. Moon Journaling

- Keep a lunar journal to track your intentions, reflections, and progress throughout the moon's phases.
- Include notes on how dinosaur archetypes influence your experiences and magickal work.

4. Combine with Elemental Magick

- Incorporate the elements (fire, earth, water, air) into your rituals to deepen your connection to the moon and prehistoric energy.

Example: Jurassic Lunar Cycle in Practice

1. **New Moon:** Set a bold intention for personal growth with T. rex energy.
2. **Waxing Crescent:** Take swift, focused action, guided by Velociraptor's agility.
3. **First Quarter:** Face challenges with T. rex determination and adaptability.
4. **Waxing Gibbous:** Refine your goals with Pterodactyl's perspective.
5. **Full Moon:** Celebrate achievements with Stegosaurus's protective energy.
6. **Waning Gibbous:** Reflect and express gratitude for the lessons learned.
7. **Last Quarter:** Release obstacles and prepare for transformation with Brontosaurus's grounding presence.
8. **Waning Crescent:** Rest and recharge, aligning with Brontosaurus energy for introspection.

Key Lessons from Jurassic Lunar Magick

1. **Cycle Awareness:** Harnessing the moon's phases helps you align your magickal practice with natural rhythms.
2. **Dynamic Energy:** Dinosaur archetypes amplify lunar energies, offering new dimensions to your rituals.
3. **Balance and Flow:** Each phase teaches a different aspect of life, from action to reflection, helping you maintain balance.
4. **Connection to the Ancient Past:** Jurassic Lunar Magick bridges the ancient and modern, grounding your work in the primal energy of dinosaurs.

Conclusion

Jurassic Lunar Magick is a transformative practice that combines the power of the moon's phases with the energy of prehistoric Earth. By aligning dinosaur archetypes with lunar cycles, you can enhance your rituals, manifest your intentions, and deepen your connection to both the cosmos and the ancient world.

Let the moonlight guide you as you walk this ancient path, empowered by the resilience and wisdom of dinosaurs. Each phase offers an opportunity to grow, adapt, and transform, carrying the strength of the Mesozoic into your spiritual practice.

Chapter 17: Rituals for Dinosaur Invocation

Dinosaurs, the ancient rulers of Earth, hold immense spiritual energy that can be summoned and incorporated into your magickal practice. Their spirits represent primal power, resilience, and the untamed forces of nature. Invoking dinosaur spirits through rituals allows you to access their wisdom, align with their unique qualities, and channel their energy for protection, strength, transformation, and spiritual growth.

This chapter provides detailed, step-by-step instructions for crafting and performing rituals to invoke dinosaur spirits and incorporate their energy into your spiritual practice.

Understanding Dinosaur Invocation

Invocation involves calling upon the essence or spirit of a dinosaur to work with its energy in a ritual or magickal setting. These spirits are archetypal energies rather than physical manifestations, representing the traits and qualities of specific dinosaurs.

Why Invoke Dinosaur Spirits?

1. **Empowerment:** Gain strength, courage, and resilience by channeling their primal energy.
2. **Guidance:** Access the wisdom of ancient Earth and prehistoric survival strategies.
3. **Protection:** Call upon their defensive traits to shield yourself or your space from harm.
4. **Spiritual Connection:** Deepen your bond with the Earth and its ancient history.

Preparing for Dinosaur Invocation
1. Create a Sacred Space

- Choose a quiet, undisturbed location for your ritual.
- Cleanse the space using smoke (sage, palo santo), sound (bells, singing bowls), or saltwater to remove negative energy.
- Set up a dinosaur altar with fossils, figurines, candles, and items that represent the dinosaur you wish to invoke.

2. Choose the Dinosaur Spirit

Select a dinosaur archetype based on your intention:

- *Tyrannosaurus Rex:* Courage, leadership, and power.
- *Stegosaurus:* Protection, resilience, and boundaries.
- *Brontosaurus:* Grounding, stability, and patience.
- *Pterodactyl:* Freedom, perspective, and spiritual ascension.
- *Velociraptor:* Agility, intellect, and adaptability.

3. Gather Ritual Tools

- **Candles:** Use colors that resonate with the dinosaur's energy (e.g., red for T. rex, green for Brontosaurus).
- **Crystals:** Select stones that amplify the dinosaur's traits (e.g., black tourmaline for protection, citrine for clarity).
- **Offerings:** Prepare symbolic offerings like herbs, stones, or small food items to honor the dinosaur spirit.

Step-by-Step Dinosaur Invocation Rituals
Ritual 1: Invoking Tyrannosaurus Rex for Courage and Power
Purpose: To summon the strength and commanding presence of the T. rex, helping you overcome challenges and assert your will.

- **Materials Needed:**
    - A red or gold candle.
    - A sharp stone or replica of a T. rex tooth or claw.
    - A piece of carnelian or tiger's eye.
    - Drum or rhythmic music (optional).
- **Steps:**
    - **Set the Mood:**
        - Light the red or gold candle and place the stone on your altar.
        - Play a rhythmic beat to invoke the primal energy of the T. rex.
    - **Focus Your Intention:**
        - Hold the sharp stone or claw in your hand and state your intention aloud, e.g., "I summon the spirit of Tyrannosaurus Rex to grant me courage and strength."
    - **Invocation:**
        - Say:

Tyrant king, ruler of old,
Mighty spirit, fierce and bold.
Grant me power, strength to lead,
Your courage flows; I take your heed.

-
    - **Channel the Energy:**
        - Visualize the T. rex standing beside you, its presence filling you with determination and fearlessness.
    - **Conclude the Ritual:**
        - Thank the T. rex spirit and extinguish the candle. Keep the stone as a talisman of courage.

Ritual 2: Invoking Stegosaurus for Protection

Purpose: To create a protective shield around yourself or your space, using the defensive energy of the Stegosaurus.

- **Materials Needed:**
    - A green or black candle.
    - A piece of black tourmaline or obsidian.
    - A Stegosaurus figurine or image.
    - Salt for a protective circle.
- **Steps:**
    - **Prepare the Space:**
        - Sprinkle a circle of salt around your ritual area.
        - Light the candle and place the Stegosaurus representation at the center.
    - **Focus Your Intention:**
        - Hold the black tourmaline and visualize a protective barrier forming around you.
    - **Invocation:**
        - Say:

Guardian Stegosaurus, shield of might,
Protect my spirit, day and night.
With plates and spikes, your strength surrounds,
No harm shall enter, no ill abounds.

-
    - **Visualize the Protection:**
        - See the Stegosaurus's plates forming an impenetrable shield around you or your space.
    - **Conclude the Ritual:**
        - Thank the spirit of the Stegosaurus, extinguish the candle, and leave the salt circle intact for continued protection.

Ritual 3: Invoking Brontosaurus for Grounding and Stability

Purpose: To ground yourself and build emotional and spiritual stability through the gentle energy of the Brontosaurus.

- **Materials Needed:**
    - A brown or green candle.
    - A piece of petrified wood or smoky quartz.
    - Soil or a small plant.
- **Steps:**
    - **Prepare the Space:**
        - Light the candle and place the soil or plant on your altar.
        - Hold the petrified wood in your hand.
    - **Focus Your Intention:**
        - Reflect on areas of your life where you seek stability and grounding.
    - **Invocation:**
        - Say:

Brontosaurus, steady and strong,
Root my spirit where I belong.
Teach me patience, strength, and grace,
Ground my energy in this sacred space.

-
    - **Visualize Grounding Energy:**
        - Imagine roots growing from your feet into the Earth, connecting you to the steady energy of the Brontosaurus.
    - **Conclude the Ritual:**
        - Thank the Brontosaurus spirit and leave the soil or plant as an offering.

Ritual 4: Invoking Pterodactyl for Freedom and Perspective

Purpose: To gain clarity, rise above challenges, and embrace spiritual freedom with the energy of the Pterodactyl.

- **Materials Needed:**
    - A white or silver candle.
    - A feather or wing-shaped object.
    - A piece of clear quartz or selenite.
- **Steps:**
    - **Prepare the Space:**
        - Light the candle and place the feather on your altar.
        - Hold the quartz in your hand.
    - **Focus Your Intention:**
        - Reflect on areas where you seek freedom or a broader perspective.
    - **Invocation:**
        - Say:

Pterodactyl, soaring high,
Lift my spirit to the sky.
Grant me vision, clear and true,
Guide my path with wisdom anew.

-
    - **Visualize Freedom:**
        - Imagine yourself flying alongside the Pterodactyl, seeing your challenges from a new perspective.
    - **Conclude the Ritual:**
        - Thank the Pterodactyl spirit and extinguish the candle. Keep the quartz as a reminder of clarity.

Post-Ritual Practices

1. **Offer Gratitude:** Always thank the dinosaur spirit for its presence and guidance.
2. **Reflect:** Write down your experiences in a journal, noting any messages, feelings, or insights.
3. **Talisman Use:** Keep the ritual tools (stones, feathers, fossils) as empowered talismans for continued connection to the invoked energy.
4. **Repeat as Needed:** Perform these rituals regularly to strengthen your connection and amplify their effects.

Key Lessons from Dinosaur Invocation

1. **Respect Ancient Energies:** Approach dinosaur spirits with reverence and gratitude for their power and wisdom.
2. **Tailor Rituals to Intentions:** Choose dinosaurs and rituals that align with your specific goals.
3. **Ground and Center:** Always ground yourself before and after rituals to maintain balance.
4. **Cultivate a Relationship:** Building a connection with dinosaur spirits over time deepens their influence in your practice.

Conclusion

Rituals for dinosaur invocation are a profound way to access the primal energy of the Earth's ancient guardians. Whether you seek courage, protection, grounding, or freedom, these spirits offer a wealth of power and wisdom to enhance your spiritual journey.

By regularly invoking dinosaur spirits, you not only draw strength and guidance from their archetypes but also forge a deeper connection to the prehistoric energy that shaped our world. Let these ancient beings guide you as you channel their power into your magickal practice and personal growth.

Chapter 18: Spells for Strength, Courage, and Resilience

Dinosaurs were masters of survival, embodying strength, courage, and resilience as they ruled the Earth for millions of years. These qualities can be channeled into practical spells to empower your life, overcome challenges, and fortify your spirit. By aligning with dinosaur archetypes, you tap into their raw, primal energy to enhance your ability to persevere, face fears, and stand strong in adversity.

This chapter provides a variety of spells using dinosaur archetypes for strength, courage, and resilience. Each spell is designed with clear steps, practical tools, and detailed explanations to ensure effective results.

Harnessing Dinosaur Archetypes for Empowerment

Each dinosaur archetype represents specific traits that can be utilized in spells for empowerment:

1. **Tyrannosaurus Rex (Strength & Leadership):** Commands power, dominance, and the ability to face challenges head-on.
2. **Stegosaurus (Protection & Resilience):** Offers grounded strength and the fortitude to withstand difficulties.
3. **Brontosaurus (Stability & Endurance):** Provides calm, steady energy to persist through prolonged challenges.
4. **Velociraptor (Agility & Courage):** Embodies quick thinking, adaptability, and bravery in uncertain situations.
5. **Pterodactyl (Freedom & Perspective):** Grants clarity, the ability to rise above fear, and a broader view of obstacles.

Spells for Strength
1. T. rex Power Surge Spell
Purpose: To summon raw strength and confidence in the face of overwhelming obstacles.

- **Materials Needed:**
    - A red or gold candle (symbolizing strength and power).
    - A small sharp stone or claw-like object (to represent T. rex energy).
    - A piece of carnelian for vitality and courage.
- **Steps:**
    - **Set the Stage:**
        - Light the candle and place the sharp stone on your altar or in your hand.
        - Hold the carnelian in your dominant hand.
    - **Focus on Strength:**
        - Close your eyes and visualize the powerful figure of a T. rex, its energy radiating strength and dominance.
    - **Chant:**

Tyrannosaurus, fearless and strong,
Lend me power to face what's wrong.
With strength that roars and courage that grows,
Through your energy, my strength flows.

-
    - **Empower Yourself:**
        - Imagine a surge of red and gold energy flowing from the T. rex into you, filling you with unstoppable strength.
    - **Seal the Spell:**
        - Allow the candle to burn down safely or extinguish it. Carry the carnelian as a talisman of strength.

2. Brontosaurus Endurance Spell

Purpose: To build resilience and sustain strength through long-term challenges.

- **Materials Needed:**
    - A brown or green candle (symbolizing stability).
    - A piece of petrified wood or smoky quartz.
    - Soil or a small plant.
- **Steps:**
    - **Ground Yourself:**
        - Sit comfortably with the soil or plant in front of you. Light the candle.
    - **Visualize Endurance:**
        - Imagine the Brontosaurus, slow-moving but steady, thriving in a prehistoric landscape.
    - **Chant:**

Brontosaurus, strong and steady,
Teach me patience; make me ready.
Through challenges vast and trials long,
Endurance grows; I am strong.

-
    - **Empower the Stone:**
        - Hold the petrified wood or quartz and visualize its energy anchoring you like deep roots.
    - **Complete the Spell:**
        - Place the stone on your altar or carry it with you for ongoing resilience.

Spells for Courage
1. Velociraptor Bold Action Spell
Purpose: To summon the courage and quick thinking needed to act decisively.

- **Materials Needed:**
  - A yellow or orange candle (representing courage and vitality).
  - A feather or small sleek object (symbolizing Velociraptor energy).
  - A piece of tiger's eye for bravery.
- **Steps:**
  - **Create the Space:**
    - Light the candle and place the feather on your altar.
    - Hold the tiger's eye in your hand.
  - **Focus on Courage:**
    - Visualize a Velociraptor moving swiftly and confidently, embodying fearless determination.
  - **Chant:**

Swift and sharp, courageous guide,
Grant me strength to stand with pride.
Velociraptor, bold and free,
Your fearless energy flows through me.

  -
    - **Visualize Success:**
      - See yourself acting with bravery and clarity in your current situation.
    - **Seal the Energy:**
      - Place the tiger's eye near your workspace or carry it as a talisman.

2. Pterodactyl Courageous Flight Spell

Purpose: To overcome fears and gain perspective, freeing yourself from emotional constraints.

- **Materials Needed:**
    - A white or silver candle (symbolizing clarity and freedom).
    - A piece of clear quartz or moonstone.
    - A small piece of paper and pen.
- **Steps:**
    - **Write Down Your Fear:**
        - On the paper, write the fear or obstacle you wish to overcome.
    - **Set the Space:**
        - Light the candle and place the quartz near it.
    - **Chant:**

Pterodactyl, soaring high,
Teach me how to touch the sky.
With fearless wings, I rise above,
Free my heart, my mind, my love.

-
    - **Burn the Fear:**
        - Safely burn the paper in the candle flame, visualizing the fear dissolving.
    - **Conclude the Spell:**
        - Thank the Pterodactyl spirit and carry the quartz as a reminder of your courage.

Spells for Resilience
1. Stegosaurus Shield Spell
Purpose: To create an energetic shield of protection and resilience against negativity.

- **Materials Needed:**
    - A green or black candle (for protection).
    - A piece of black tourmaline or obsidian.
    - A Stegosaurus figurine or image.
- **Steps:**
    - **Set the Space:**
        - Light the candle and place the figurine or image at the center of your altar.
    - **Focus on Resilience:**
        - Visualize the plates and spikes of a Stegosaurus forming a protective barrier around you.
    - **Chant:**

Stegosaurus, shield of might,
Guard my spirit, day and night.
With spikes of steel and plates of stone,
Protect my soul; I stand alone.

-
    - **Empower the Stone:**
        - Hold the tourmaline or obsidian and visualize it absorbing negativity.
    - **Seal the Spell:**
        - Allow the candle to burn down safely or extinguish it. Keep the stone as a talisman of protection.

Enhancing Your Dinosaur Spells

1. **Combine Archetypes:** Use multiple dinosaur archetypes to blend their energies for more complex intentions.
2. **Incorporate Fossils:** Add fossils, petrified wood, or replicas to your rituals for a tangible connection to prehistoric energy.
3. **Visualize the Dinosaur's Environment:** Imagine the prehistoric landscapes where these creatures thrived, amplifying your connection to their energy.
4. **Repeat as Needed:** Revisit these spells regularly to maintain their effects or adjust them for evolving challenges.

Key Lessons from Dinosaur Spells

1. **Strength Comes from Within:** Dinosaurs teach us to harness our own innate power and resilience.
2. **Courage is a Choice:** Like Velociraptor or Pterodactyl, bravery involves facing challenges with determination and clarity.
3. **Resilience is Built Over Time:** Grounding practices, like invoking Brontosaurus energy, help you weather prolonged difficulties.
4. **Protection is Active:** Stegosaurus energy reminds us that creating boundaries is an ongoing act of self-care.

Conclusion

Spells for strength, courage, and resilience channel the unmatched power of dinosaur archetypes into your magickal practice. By aligning with their primal energy, you can overcome obstacles, face fears, and build an unshakable foundation for personal growth.

Let these ancient guardians inspire and empower you as you navigate life's challenges, drawing on their wisdom and might to create the life you desire. With these spells, the strength of the prehistoric world becomes your ally in every step of your journey.

Chapter 19: Communicating with Prehistoric Spirits

Dinosaurs, though long extinct, have left an indelible mark on the Earth. Their energy and presence can still be felt in the spiritual realm, where their primal force, resilience, and ancient wisdom endure. Communicating with prehistoric spirits allows you to access this ancient energy, gaining insight, guidance, and empowerment for your spiritual path. Through meditation, divination, and intentional rituals, you can forge a connection with the spiritual remnants of dinosaurs and invite their wisdom into your life.

This chapter provides step-by-step methods for contacting and working with prehistoric spirits, offering tools for meditation, divination, and symbolic interpretation.

Understanding Prehistoric Spirits

Prehistoric spirits are the energetic imprints or archetypal energies of dinosaurs and the ecosystems in which they thrived. They represent not only the physical presence of these creatures but also the enduring spiritual essence of their qualities:

1. **Strength and Survival:** Dinosaurs symbolize resilience and the ability to adapt to harsh environments.
2. **Primal Wisdom:** They carry the essence of the Earth's ancient knowledge and cycles.
3. **Connection to Nature:** Their spirits embody harmony with the land, emphasizing grounding and ecological balance.

By working with these spirits, you tap into a reservoir of ancient energy that can empower your spiritual practice.

Preparing to Communicate with Prehistoric Spirits
1. Create a Sacred Space

- Choose a quiet location where you can focus without interruptions.
- Cleanse the space with sage, palo santo, or incense to remove stagnant energy.
- Include fossils, stones, or dinosaur representations on your altar to anchor the energy of prehistoric spirits.

2. Set Your Intention

- Clearly define why you wish to communicate with prehistoric spirits. Examples:
    - Seeking guidance for personal challenges.
    - Tapping into their strength for resilience.
    - Understanding the cycles of life and nature.

3. Gather Tools

- **Crystals:** Use petrified wood, ammonite, or black tourmaline to facilitate grounding and connection.
- **Divination Tools:** Tarot cards, pendulums, or rune stones can serve as mediums for communication.
- **Fossils or Symbols:** Incorporate items that represent dinosaurs to act as a focus for your intention.

Meditation for Connecting with Prehistoric Spirits

Meditation is a powerful way to attune yourself to the presence of prehistoric spirits. The following guided meditation can help you establish a connection.

Step-by-Step Guided Meditation

1. **Preparation:**
    - Sit comfortably in your sacred space.
    - Place a fossil or symbolic representation of a dinosaur in your hands or nearby.
    - Light a candle and some grounding incense, such as sandalwood or frankincense.
2. **Ground Yourself:**
    - Close your eyes and take deep breaths. Visualize roots extending from your body into the Earth, anchoring you firmly to the ground.
    - Feel the ancient energy of the Earth rising through these roots, filling you with stability.
3. **Enter the Prehistoric World:**
    - Imagine yourself walking through a prehistoric landscape. See the towering trees, hear the sounds of distant creatures, and feel the raw, untamed energy of the land.
    - Visualize a dinosaur emerging from this world—a spirit guide chosen for you.
4. **Communicate with the Spirit:**
    - Greet the spirit and state your intention. For example:

Spirit of ancient strength and wisdom,
I seek your guidance and energy.
Share with me the lessons of your time,
So I may walk my path with courage and clarity.

-
    - Listen for any messages or impressions the spirit shares with you. These may come as images, words, or emotions.

1. **Express Gratitude:**
    - Thank the spirit for its guidance and presence.
    - Visualize the prehistoric landscape fading as you return to your current surroundings.
2. **Record Your Experience:**
    - Write down any insights or messages you received in a journal.

Divination Techniques for Contacting Prehistoric Spirits

Divination tools can serve as mediums for prehistoric spirits to communicate their messages. Below are methods tailored to this practice:

1. Fossil Scrying

- Use a fossil as a scrying tool to receive insights from prehistoric spirits.
    - **Steps:**
        1. Hold the fossil in your hands and set your intention for guidance.
        2. Gaze into the patterns, cracks, or textures of the fossil.
        3. Allow images, thoughts, or feelings to emerge and interpret them as messages from the spirit.

2. Pendulum Communication

- A pendulum can act as a direct line to prehistoric spirits, offering yes/no answers to your questions.
    - **Steps:**
        1. Hold the pendulum over a fossil or dinosaur representation.
        2. Ask questions, starting with simple ones to establish a connection (e.g., "Are you here to guide me?").
        3. Observe the pendulum's movement and interpret the responses.

3. Tarot or Oracle Cards

- Use a deck of cards to interpret messages from prehistoric spirits.
    - **Steps:**
        1. Shuffle the deck while focusing on your intention.
        2. Draw a card or spread and interpret it through the lens of dinosaur archetypes.
        3. Consider how the card's imagery or meaning relates to the spirit's energy.

Ritual for Invoking Prehistoric Spirits

This ritual creates a sacred connection with prehistoric spirits, allowing their energy and wisdom to flow into your life.

Materials Needed:

- A fossil, petrified wood, or symbolic item.
- A white or green candle (for spiritual clarity and grounding).
- A bowl of soil or Earth.
- Incense (sandalwood or myrrh).

Steps:

1. **Prepare the Space:**
    - Light the candle and incense. Place the fossil and bowl of soil on your altar.
2. **Set Your Intention:**
    - Hold the fossil in your hands and state your intention. For example:

Spirits of the ancient Earth, I call to thee.
Through this fossil, connect with me.
Share your wisdom, your strength, your might,
Guide my path with your primal light.

1. **Invoke the Spirit:**
    - Close your eyes and visualize the fossil glowing with ancient energy. See the spirit of a dinosaur emerging, its presence filling the room.
2. **Communicate:**
    - Ask your questions or seek guidance. Listen for responses in your mind or observe impressions around you.
3. **Seal the Connection:**
    - Thank the spirit for its guidance and ask it to return when called upon. Say:

Spirit of the past, I honor you now.
Your wisdom guides; I make this vow:
To walk in strength, with courage and grace,
Until we meet again in this sacred space.

1. **Conclude the Ritual:**
    - Extinguish the candle and incense. Leave the fossil on your altar as a charged artifact.

Signs of Prehistoric Spirit Communication

1. **Vivid Imagery:** Clear mental images or visions of prehistoric landscapes and creatures.
2. **Strong Emotions:** Feelings of awe, strength, or connection during rituals.
3. **Physical Sensations:** Warmth, tingling, or a sense of presence around you.
4. **Unusual Synchronicities:** Encounters with dinosaur symbols, fossils, or related imagery in daily life.

Incorporating Prehistoric Spirits into Daily Practice

1. **Carry a Talisman:** Keep a fossil or dinosaur symbol with you to maintain a connection with the spirit.
2. **Daily Meditation:** Spend a few minutes each day visualizing the prehistoric spirit and inviting its energy into your life.
3. **Dream Work:** Place a fossil under your pillow and set the intention to meet the spirit in your dreams.
4. **Offerings:** Leave small offerings (herbs, stones, or symbolic items) on your altar to honor the spirit.

Key Lessons from Prehistoric Spirits

1. **Resilience Through Adversity:** Dinosaurs thrived for millions of years, teaching the power of endurance and adaptability.
2. **Harmony with Nature:** Their spirits emphasize the importance of living in balance with the natural world.
3. **Ancient Wisdom:** Connecting with these spirits provides insight into the primal forces that shape life and survival.
4. **Strength in Connection:** By working with prehistoric spirits, you gain access to a deep well of spiritual support and empowerment.

Conclusion

Communicating with prehistoric spirits allows you to bridge the gap between the ancient past and the present, inviting the strength, wisdom, and resilience of dinosaurs into your spiritual practice. Through meditation, divination, and intentional rituals, you can build a powerful connection with these timeless beings, gaining guidance and empowerment for your journey.

Let the spirits of the ancient Earth guide you with their enduring energy, reminding you of the boundless strength and adaptability that lies within us all.

Chapter 20: Dino Dreams and Shamanic Journeying

Dinosaurs, as archetypes of resilience, primal power, and ancient wisdom, often emerge in dreams and shamanic journeys to deliver messages and guidance. These encounters bridge the conscious and subconscious realms, connecting you to Earth's prehistoric energies and offering insights into personal transformation, spiritual growth, and your connection to nature.

In this chapter, we explore how to interpret dinosaur appearances in dreams, how to facilitate shamanic journeys to connect with their spirits, and the transformative lessons these encounters can bring.

Dino Dreams: Messages from the Subconscious

Dreams featuring dinosaurs often carry deep spiritual or psychological meaning. These prehistoric beings act as symbols of ancient power, forgotten wisdom, or unresolved fears. Understanding their role in dreams helps unlock the messages they deliver.

Common Dinosaur Dream Themes and Their Meanings

1. **Being Chased by a Dinosaur**
    - **Interpretation:** Facing fears or unresolved issues. The dinosaur may represent a challenge or emotion you've been avoiding.
    - **Message:** It's time to confront what you've been running from and harness your inner strength.
2. **Discovering Dinosaur Fossils**
    - **Interpretation:** Unearthing hidden truths or ancient wisdom. Fossils symbolize aspects of yourself or your heritage that are waiting to be rediscovered.
    - **Message:** Dig deeper into your past or spiritual practice to uncover valuable insights.
3. **Riding or Befriending a Dinosaur**
    - **Interpretation:** Mastering primal energy and aligning with ancient strength. This symbolizes a harmonious connection with powerful forces in your life.
    - **Message:** Trust your abilities to navigate challenges and embrace your inner power.
4. **Dinosaurs in a Prehistoric Landscape**
    - **Interpretation:** Connecting with the primal Earth and your instinctual self. The landscape often represents your subconscious mind or untapped potential.
    - **Message:** Embrace your natural instincts and reconnect with your authentic self.
5. **Witnessing a Dinosaur's Extinction**
    - **Interpretation:** Letting go of outdated beliefs, habits, or situations. The extinction event signifies transformation and renewal.
    - **Message:** Release what no longer serves you to make way for new growth.

How to Encourage Dino Dreams

To invite dinosaurs into your dreams, use these techniques:

1. **Set Your Intention:** Before bed, state your intention to dream of dinosaurs or receive their guidance. For example:
    - "I invite the spirits of the ancient Earth to visit me in my dreams and share their wisdom."
2. **Create a Dream Altar:**
    - Place fossils, dinosaur figurines, or symbolic items near your bed.
    - Light a candle or burn incense with grounding scents like cedarwood or myrrh.
3. **Use Crystals:**
    - Place petrified wood, ammonite, or moonstone under your pillow to enhance dream recall and spiritual connection.
4. **Keep a Dream Journal:**
    - Record your dreams immediately upon waking. Look for recurring symbols, themes, or emotions associated with dinosaurs.

Shamanic Journeying: Entering the Prehistoric Realm

Shamanic journeying is a meditative practice that allows you to travel to non-ordinary realities to meet spiritual allies, including dinosaur spirits. These journeys offer a deeper connection to prehistoric energies, helping you access guidance and transformation.

The Three Worlds in Shamanic Practice

1. **Lower World:** The realm of Earth spirits and ancestors, where dinosaur spirits often reside. This is a place of grounding, primal energy, and personal transformation.
2. **Middle World:** The spiritual aspect of our physical world, where you may encounter dinosaurs as guardians of specific landscapes.
3. **Upper World:** The ethereal realm of higher guidance and celestial wisdom. Flying dinosaurs like Pterodactyls often appear here, symbolizing ascension and perspective.

Preparing for a Shamanic Journey

1. **Set Your Intention:**
    - Clearly define your purpose for journeying. Examples:
        - "I seek to connect with the spirit of a dinosaur for guidance on resilience."
        - "I wish to learn from the ancient wisdom of the Earth."
2. **Create a Sacred Space:**
    - Cleanse the area with sage, palo santo, or sound.
    - Place fossils, crystals, or symbolic items on your altar.
3. **Use Drumming or Rhythmic Sound:**
    - Drumming, rattling, or rhythmic music helps shift your consciousness into the trance state needed for journeying.
4. **Gather Tools:**
    - Include a blindfold or eye mask, a journal for recording insights, and a comfortable place to lie or sit.

Step-by-Step Shamanic Journey to Connect with Dinosaur Spirits

1. **Relax and Ground Yourself:**
    - Sit or lie down in your sacred space. Close your eyes and focus on your breath. Imagine roots extending from your body into the Earth, anchoring you.
2. **Visualize Your Entry Point:**
    - Picture a natural portal, such as a cave, tree hollow, or river, that leads to the Lower World.
3. **Journey to the Prehistoric Realm:**
    - Enter the portal and visualize yourself descending into a lush, prehistoric landscape. Observe the sights, sounds, and sensations.
4. **Meet the Dinosaur Spirit:**
    - Allow a dinosaur spirit to approach you. This may be a specific species or a general archetype. Trust your intuition in recognizing its presence.
5. **Communicate:**
    - Greet the spirit and ask your questions or seek guidance. For example:
        - "What strength do I need to overcome my current challenges?"
        - "How can I embody resilience and adaptability?"
6. **Receive Messages:**
    - Be open to visual, auditory, or emotional impressions. The spirit may offer direct answers, symbolic imagery, or energetic sensations.
7. **Return to Your World:**
    - Thank the dinosaur spirit for its guidance. Retrace your steps back through the portal and slowly return to your physical awareness.
8. **Record Your Experience:**
    - Write down everything you saw, felt, and heard. Reflect on how the guidance applies to your life.

Signs of Dinosaur Spirits in Shamanic Journeys

1. **Powerful Physical Presence:** The dinosaur spirit may appear as a towering figure, representing strength and protection.
2. **Elemental Connections:** You may feel a strong connection to Earth, fire, water, or air, reflecting the spirit's domain.
3. **Symbolic Behavior:** The dinosaur's actions—e.g., protecting you, leading you, or showing you specific paths—offer clues to its message.

Incorporating Dino Guidance into Your Life

1. **Create a Dino Spirit Altar:**
    - Dedicate a space to honor the spirit, including fossils, crystals, and candles.
2. **Daily Affirmations:**
    - Use affirmations inspired by the spirit's message. For example:
        - "I stand strong like the T. rex, unshaken by challenges."
        - "I flow with change like the currents of the prehistoric seas."
3. **Symbolic Talismans:**
    - Carry a fossil or stone as a reminder of the spirit's guidance and protection.
4. **Dream and Journey Follow-Up:**
    - Continue journaling your experiences and revisiting the spirit through dreams or shamanic journeys to deepen the connection.

Key Lessons from Dino Dreams and Shamanic Journeys

1. **Primal Strength:** Dinosaurs remind us of our inner power and ability to adapt to challenges.
2. **Ancient Wisdom:** Their presence connects us to the cycles of nature and the enduring resilience of life.
3. **Intuitive Guidance:** Dreams and journeys provide symbolic messages tailored to your spiritual path.
4. **Connection to Earth:** Working with dinosaur spirits deepens your relationship with the natural world and its ancient energies.

Conclusion

Dino dreams and shamanic journeying offer profound opportunities to connect with prehistoric spirits, gaining access to their strength, wisdom, and transformative energy. Whether they appear in your dreams to offer symbolic messages or guide you through shamanic landscapes, these ancient beings serve as powerful allies on your spiritual journey.

By embracing their lessons and integrating their guidance into your life, you align with the timeless resilience and primal energy of Earth's ancient past, empowering you to navigate the challenges and transformations of the present.

Chapter 21: Using Dinosaur Energy for Transformation

Dinosaurs embody resilience, evolution, and transformation. They thrived in a constantly changing world, adapting to shifting climates and landscapes for millions of years. Even their extinction marked a profound transformation, giving rise to new lifeforms and ecosystems. Harnessing dinosaur energy allows you to tap into this ancient wisdom to catalyze personal and spiritual growth, embrace change, and emerge stronger from life's challenges.

In this chapter, you'll learn how to channel dinosaur energy for transformation, explore its symbolic significance, and practice rituals and techniques to facilitate your journey toward growth and renewal.

The Transformative Power of Dinosaurs

Dinosaurs represent transformation on multiple levels:

1. **Adaptation and Survival:** Their ability to evolve and thrive for millions of years demonstrates the power of adaptability and resilience in the face of adversity.
2. **Cycles of Life and Death:** The extinction of dinosaurs symbolizes the natural cycles of endings and beginnings, teaching us to embrace change as a pathway to growth.
3. **Primal Energy:** As ancient beings, dinosaurs embody raw, untamed energy that can ignite profound transformation when properly harnessed.

By invoking these qualities, you align with the energy of transformation, enabling you to break through limitations, release the old, and welcome the new.

Preparing for Transformation with Dinosaur Energy

1. Understand Your Intentions

Before working with dinosaur energy, clarify what aspect of your life you wish to transform:

- Are you seeking personal growth, such as overcoming fear or building confidence?
- Do you want to heal emotional wounds or release past trauma?
- Are you ready to step into a new phase of your spiritual journey?

2. Choose a Dinosaur Archetype

Each dinosaur archetype offers unique qualities that align with specific types of transformation:

- **Tyrannosaurus Rex:** For strength, courage, and breaking through limitations.
- **Brontosaurus:** For grounding, patience, and steady progress.
- **Stegosaurus:** For protection and establishing boundaries during times of change.
- **Pterodactyl:** For gaining perspective and rising above challenges.
- **Velociraptor:** For agility and adaptability in navigating new situations.

3. Create a Sacred Space

Set up an altar or dedicated space with items that resonate with your transformation goals:

- **Fossils or Dinosaur Representations:** Symbols of the dinosaur energy you wish to invoke.
- **Crystals:** Use stones like obsidian for releasing negativity, clear quartz for clarity, and carnelian for motivation.
- **Candles:** Choose colors that align with your intentions, such as red for strength, green for renewal, or white for clarity.

Techniques for Harnessing Dinosaur Energy
1. Visualization for Transformation

Visualization is a powerful way to connect with dinosaur energy and channel it into your intentions.

1. **Relax and Ground Yourself:**
   - Sit in a comfortable position and take deep breaths to calm your mind.
   - Imagine roots extending from your body into the Earth, grounding you.
2. **Call Upon the Dinosaur Archetype:**
   - Visualize the dinosaur whose energy aligns with your transformation. For example:
     - See a *Tyrannosaurus Rex* smashing through obstacles, symbolizing your strength to overcome challenges.
     - Picture a *Pterodactyl* soaring above the landscape, representing your ability to gain clarity and perspective.
3. **Absorb the Energy:**
   - Imagine the dinosaur's energy flowing into you, filling you with courage, resilience, or insight.
   - Visualize yourself embodying its qualities as you move toward transformation.
4. **Affirmation:**
   - Repeat a mantra or affirmation that reinforces your intention, such as:

I embrace the power of transformation.
With the strength of [dinosaur], I grow and evolve.

2. Ritual for Releasing the Old

This ritual helps you let go of habits, emotions, or situations that no longer serve you, paving the way for transformation.

1. **Materials Needed:**
    - A black candle (symbolizing release).
    - A fossil or symbolic dinosaur item.
    - A piece of paper and a pen.
    - A fireproof bowl.
2. **Steps:**
    - **Set Your Intention:**
        - Write down what you wish to release on the piece of paper.
    - **Invoke Dinosaur Energy:**
        - Light the black candle and hold the fossil in your hands.
        - Say:

Ancient spirit of transformation, hear my call.
Guide me as I release the old and embrace the new.

-
    - **Burn the Paper:**
        - Safely burn the paper in the fireproof bowl, visualizing the dinosaur's energy helping you release the burden.
    - **Conclude the Ritual:**
        - Extinguish the candle and thank the dinosaur spirit for its guidance.

3. Ritual for Embracing the New

This ritual aligns you with the energy of renewal, helping you step into a new phase with confidence and clarity.

1. **Materials Needed:**
   - A green or white candle (symbolizing growth and clarity).
   - A crystal, such as clear quartz or citrine.
   - A small plant or seedling (optional).
2. **Steps:**
   - **Prepare the Space:**
     - Light the candle and place the crystal and plant on your altar.
   - **Visualize Your Goal:**
     - Close your eyes and visualize the new phase or goal you're stepping into. Imagine the dinosaur archetype walking beside you, supporting your journey.
   - **Chant:**

Spirit of [dinosaur], strong and wise,
Guide my steps as I rise.
With your power, I am renewed,
Transformed, aligned, and imbued.

- - **Empower the Crystal:**
     - Hold the crystal and imagine it absorbing the energy of your intention. Keep it with you as a talisman of transformation.
   - **Conclude the Ritual:**
     - Thank the dinosaur spirit and extinguish the candle.

Incorporating Dinosaur Energy into Daily Life

1. **Carry Talismans:** Keep a fossil, crystal, or dinosaur symbol with you to maintain a connection to transformative energy.
2. **Use Affirmations:** Create affirmations inspired by the dinosaur archetype you're working with, such as:
   - "I am strong and fearless, like the Tyrannosaurus Rex."
   - "I grow steadily and with grace, like the Brontosaurus."
3. **Practice Gratitude:** Regularly honor the dinosaur spirits and their guidance by leaving small offerings on your altar.

Signs of Transformation Through Dinosaur Energy

1. **Increased Resilience:** You feel more capable of handling challenges and adapting to change.
2. **New Opportunities:** Doors open for growth in areas you've been focusing on.
3. **Emotional Release:** You experience a sense of relief or freedom after letting go of old patterns.
4. **Spiritual Awakening:** You feel a deeper connection to the natural world and your inner power.

Key Lessons from Dinosaur Transformation

1. **Embrace Change:** Dinosaurs teach us that transformation is a natural part of life, essential for growth and renewal.
2. **Harness Strength:** Their primal energy reminds us of our inner power to overcome obstacles.
3. **Trust the Process:** Just as dinosaurs adapted over time, trust that your transformation will unfold as it's meant to.
4. **Stay Grounded:** Transformation is most effective when rooted in a solid foundation, like the steady presence of a Brontosaurus.

Conclusion

Using dinosaur energy for transformation is a profound way to align with the primal forces of nature and empower your personal and spiritual growth. By working with the unique qualities of each dinosaur archetype, you can break through limitations, release the old, and embrace new possibilities with strength and resilience.

Let the ancient wisdom of dinosaurs guide you through life's changes, helping you evolve into your highest potential. With their energy, transformation becomes not only possible but inevitable, leading you to greater empowerment and harmony.

Chapter 22: The Magick of Extinction and Renewal

Extinction, though often viewed as an end, is a natural part of the cycles of life. For dinosaurs, their mass extinction marked the end of an era, but it also paved the way for new species to evolve, leading to the Earth as we know it today. This profound cycle of extinction and renewal carries deep spiritual lessons, teaching us the importance of letting go, embracing change, and allowing transformation to unfold.

In this chapter, we delve into the magick of extinction and renewal, exploring how to work with dinosaur energy to release the old, invite new beginnings, and align with the natural rhythms of life and rebirth.

The Spiritual Lessons of Extinction

Extinction symbolizes more than just an ending; it represents a powerful spiritual process:

1. **Releasing the Old:** Extinction teaches us that certain things—whether habits, relationships, or beliefs—must end to make room for growth.
2. **The Cycle of Change:** Life is cyclical, and endings are an integral part of transformation and renewal.
3. **Acceptance of Impermanence:** Dinosaurs remind us that even the most powerful forces must sometimes yield, emphasizing the beauty of impermanence.

By embracing the energy of extinction, we learn to let go gracefully, trusting that renewal will follow.

The Spiritual Lessons of Renewal

Renewal is the counterpart to extinction, symbolizing new beginnings and fresh opportunities:

1. **Emergence of New Life:** Just as mammals thrived after the dinosaurs, renewal brings new possibilities after endings.
2. **Rebirth Through Transformation:** Renewal is not simply starting over—it's evolving into something stronger, wiser, and more aligned with your purpose.
3. **Resilience and Growth:** Renewal teaches us to rise from challenges, carrying the lessons of the past into the future.

Harnessing the energy of renewal helps you navigate transitions with hope, resilience, and a sense of purpose.

Dinosaur Archetypes and the Cycle of Extinction and Renewal

Dinosaurs exemplify the balance between extinction and renewal, each archetype embodying unique qualities for navigating this cycle:

- **Tyrannosaurus Rex:** The power to destroy old patterns, clearing the way for transformation.
- **Brontosaurus:** Steady, grounded energy to navigate the transition from loss to renewal.
- **Stegosaurus:** Protective strength to help you release what no longer serves you while shielding your core.
- **Velociraptor:** Adaptability and agility to thrive in new environments after change.
- **Pterodactyl:** The ability to rise above endings and see the broader perspective of renewal.

Rituals for Embracing Extinction and Renewal
1. Ritual for Releasing the Old (Extinction Energy)

This ritual helps you consciously let go of what no longer serves you, aligning with the transformative energy of extinction.

- **Materials Needed:**
  - A black candle (symbolizing endings).
  - A piece of obsidian or smoky quartz.
  - A piece of paper and pen.
  - A fireproof bowl.
- **Steps:**
  - **Set Your Intention:**
    - Write down what you wish to release (e.g., limiting beliefs, toxic relationships, or old habits).
  - **Invoke Extinction Energy:**
    - Light the black candle and hold the obsidian or smoky quartz.
    - Say:

Spirits of the ancient Earth, I call to thee,
Guide me in this act of release.
Like the dinosaurs, I let the old fall away,
Clearing the path for a brighter day.

-
  - **Burn the Paper:**
    - Safely burn the paper in the fireproof bowl, visualizing the energy dissolving and freeing you.
  - **Thank the Energy:**
    - Extinguish the candle and thank the dinosaur spirit for its guidance.

2. Ritual for Inviting Renewal

This ritual channels renewal energy, helping you step into new beginnings with clarity and purpose.

- **Materials Needed:**
    - A green or white candle (symbolizing growth and renewal).
    - A small plant or seedling (optional).
    - A clear quartz or citrine crystal.
- **Steps:**
    - **Prepare the Space:**
        - Light the green or white candle and place the plant or crystal in front of you.
    - **Set Your Intention:**
        - Focus on what you wish to invite into your life, such as new opportunities, healing, or personal growth.
    - **Invoke Renewal Energy:**
        - Hold the crystal and say:

Spirit of renewal, ancient and wise,
Guide my path as I rise.
From the ashes, I am reborn,
With strength anew, I greet the morn.

   -
     - **Visualize Growth:**
        - Imagine yourself thriving in this new phase, much like life emerging after an extinction event.
     - **Conclude the Ritual:**
        - Thank the energy, extinguish the candle, and keep the crystal or plant as a symbol of renewal.

Shamanic Journey for Extinction and Renewal

Shamanic journeying can help you explore the deeper meanings of extinction and renewal by connecting with dinosaur spirits.

Steps:

1. **Set Your Intention:**
    - Clearly define whether you are seeking to release the old (extinction) or embrace the new (renewal).
2. **Enter the Journey:**
    - Visualize yourself in a prehistoric landscape, with dinosaurs representing either endings or new beginnings.
3. **Communicate with the Spirits:**
    - Ask for guidance on what to release or how to step into renewal.
4. **Return and Reflect:**
    - Journal your insights and how they apply to your transformation.

Incorporating Extinction and Renewal Energy into Daily Life

1. **Daily Affirmations:**
    - For extinction: "I release what no longer serves me with grace and trust in the process."
    - For renewal: "I welcome new beginnings with strength and purpose."
2. **Symbolic Items:**
    - Carry a fossil or crystal as a reminder of the cycle of extinction and renewal.
3. **Regular Reflection:**
    - Periodically review what you've released and what you've gained, noting how transformation has shaped your path.

Key Lessons from the Magick of Extinction and Renewal

1. **Endings Are Beginnings:** The extinction of dinosaurs led to the rise of new life, reminding us that every ending creates space for growth.
2. **Release with Grace:** Letting go is not a loss but a gift, allowing new opportunities to take root.
3. **Embrace Change:** Renewal is a natural and necessary part of life, empowering us to evolve and thrive.
4. **Trust the Cycle:** Like the cycles of life, death, and rebirth in nature, trust that your journey will unfold as it should.

Conclusion

The magick of extinction and renewal teaches us to embrace the cycles of life with courage and grace. By working with dinosaur energy, you align with ancient wisdom, empowering yourself to release the past, step into the future, and transform into your fullest potential.

Let the spirit of the dinosaurs guide you through these cycles, reminding you that even the mightiest forces must yield to change, and in doing so, create space for something even greater to emerge.

Chapter 23: Balancing Power and Wisdom with Brachiosaurus

The Brachiosaurus, a towering herbivore of the Jurassic Era, represents a harmonious balance of strength and serenity. Despite its massive size and immense power, the Brachiosaurus thrived through patience, wisdom, and adaptability, rather than aggression. This gentle giant serves as a spiritual guide for those seeking to balance power with wisdom, achieve harmony, and cultivate long-term success in their magickal practices.

In this chapter, we explore the spiritual symbolism of the Brachiosaurus, its lessons for balancing strength and patience, and rituals and techniques to work with its energy for personal and spiritual growth.

The Spiritual Symbolism of Brachiosaurus

The Brachiosaurus offers profound lessons in power, wisdom, and harmony:

1. **Strength in Stillness:** Its towering form symbolizes immense power, but its gentle demeanor reminds us that true strength often lies in restraint and wisdom.
2. **Patience and Longevity:** As a long-lived species that thrived on slow, deliberate actions, the Brachiosaurus teaches us the value of patience and long-term thinking.
3. **Harmony with Nature:** As a peaceful herbivore, it embodies balance and coexistence, offering guidance for achieving harmony in both life and magickal practice.
4. **Connection to Higher Realms:** With its long neck reaching toward the sky, the Brachiosaurus symbolizes a connection to higher wisdom and spiritual awareness.

Key Lessons from Brachiosaurus Energy

1. **Balance Power with Wisdom:** Use your strength thoughtfully, ensuring it aligns with your higher purpose.
2. **Embrace Patience:** Success often requires steady progress and the willingness to wait for the right timing.
3. **Live in Harmony:** Seek balance in your relationships, environment, and spiritual practices.
4. **Reach Higher:** Aim for spiritual growth and higher understanding, much like the Brachiosaurus reaching for sustenance in the treetops.

Rituals for Working with Brachiosaurus Energy
1. Grounding and Harmonizing Ritual
This ritual helps you achieve inner harmony and balance your physical, emotional, and spiritual energies.

- **Materials Needed:**
  - A green or brown candle (symbolizing balance and grounding).
  - A piece of petrified wood or moss agate.
  - A bowl of soil or sand.
- **Steps:**
  - **Set the Space:**
    - Light the candle and place the soil bowl on your altar.
    - Hold the petrified wood or moss agate in your hands.
  - **Invoke Brachiosaurus Energy:**
    - Close your eyes and visualize the gentle, towering figure of a Brachiosaurus moving peacefully through its environment.
    - Say:

Brachiosaurus, wise and strong,
Guide me where I belong.
Balance my power, align my soul,
Help me reach my highest goal.

  -
    - **Ground Yourself:**
      - Imagine roots extending from your feet into the Earth, anchoring you to stability while connecting you to the Brachiosaurus's calm and steady energy.
    - **Visualize Harmony:**
      - See the different aspects of your life (work, relationships, spiritual practice) aligning in perfect balance.
    - **Conclude:**
      - Thank the Brachiosaurus spirit and extinguish the candle. Keep the petrified wood or moss agate as a talisman of balance.

2. Patience and Long-Term Success Spell

This spell aligns you with the patience and perseverance of the Brachiosaurus to achieve long-term goals.

- **Materials Needed:**
    - A blue or green candle (representing patience and growth).
    - A leaf or piece of bark.
    - A piece of amethyst (symbolizing wisdom).
    - A journal or piece of paper.
- **Steps:**
    - **Define Your Goal:**
        - Write down a long-term goal you wish to achieve, along with the steps required to reach it.
    - **Set the Space:**
        - Light the candle and place the leaf, bark, or amethyst on your altar.
    - **Invoke Brachiosaurus Energy:**
        - Hold the amethyst and say:

Brachiosaurus, patient and wise,
Teach me to see with steady eyes.
Help me to wait, to grow, to thrive,
As I work toward dreams alive.

-
    - **Visualize Growth:**
        - Picture your goal as a towering tree, growing steadily as you nurture it with your actions.
    - **Seal the Spell:**
        - Place the leaf or bark in your journal next to your written goal as a reminder of the Brachiosaurus's guidance.

3. Connection to Higher Wisdom Meditation

This meditation helps you tap into the higher wisdom of the Brachiosaurus for spiritual growth and enlightenment.

- **Steps:**
  1. **Relax and Ground Yourself:**
     - Sit comfortably in your sacred space. Close your eyes and take slow, deep breaths.
  2. **Visualize the Brachiosaurus:**
     - Imagine yourself in a lush prehistoric forest. A Brachiosaurus appears, towering above the trees, its gaze calm and wise.
  3. **Climb the Brachiosaurus:**
     - Picture yourself climbing its neck, each step taking you closer to the sky. As you ascend, feel your perspective shifting and your understanding deepening.
  4. **Receive Wisdom:**
     - At the top, ask the Brachiosaurus for guidance. Listen for messages in the form of thoughts, feelings, or visions.
  5. **Return:**
     - Descend gently, bringing the wisdom back with you. Reflect on your experience and journal any insights.

Daily Practices to Align with Brachiosaurus Energy

1. **Affirmations:**
   - Use affirmations to embody Brachiosaurus energy:
     - "I balance power with wisdom and patience."
     - "I grow steadily toward my goals, trusting the process."
2. **Symbolic Items:**
   - Carry a small fossil, stone, or leaf as a reminder of the Brachiosaurus's qualities.
3. **Nature Walks:**
   - Spend time in nature, observing the slow, steady growth of trees and plants. Reflect on the Brachiosaurus's harmony with its environment.
4. **Mindful Decisions:**
   - Before taking action, ask yourself, "Am I acting with wisdom and patience?"

Signs of Connection with Brachiosaurus Energy

1. **Calm Strength:** You feel a steady, grounded confidence in your decisions and actions.
2. **Increased Patience:** You find yourself more willing to wait for the right timing or approach challenges methodically.
3. **Harmonious Growth:** Your goals and spiritual practice align seamlessly, progressing steadily without force.
4. **Heightened Wisdom:** You gain clarity and insight, often seeing the bigger picture in challenging situations.

Key Lessons from Brachiosaurus

1. **Power Must Be Balanced:** True strength comes from the wisdom to use power thoughtfully and harmoniously.
2. **Patience Yields Growth:** Like the slow movements of the Brachiosaurus, lasting success comes from deliberate and steady effort.
3. **Harmony is Key:** Balance is essential in every aspect of life—between strength and gentleness, action and rest, and the physical and spiritual.
4. **Reach Higher:** Always strive for growth and understanding, reaching beyond the immediate to grasp higher wisdom.

Conclusion

The Brachiosaurus teaches us that strength and wisdom are not opposing forces but complementary aspects of a balanced life. By working with its energy, you can cultivate harmony, patience, and long-term success in your magickal practices and personal growth.

Let the gentle giant of the Jurassic guide you, helping you balance power with restraint, ambition with patience, and groundedness with the pursuit of higher wisdom. With the Brachiosaurus as your ally, you can achieve lasting success while remaining rooted in harmony and grace.

Chapter 24: Dinosaur Guardians of the Astral Plane

The astral plane is a vast and multifaceted realm where consciousness transcends physical boundaries. While this realm offers profound opportunities for exploration, learning, and spiritual growth, it also holds potential risks from unbalanced energies and intrusive entities. Enlisting dinosaur spirits as guardians during astral travel provides a layer of protection, drawing on their primal strength, resilience, and ancient wisdom.

In this chapter, you'll learn how to work with dinosaur spirits as protectors, set up safeguards for your astral journeys, and deepen your connection with these powerful allies to ensure safe and transformative psychic exploration.

Why Choose Dinosaur Spirits as Astral Guardians?

Dinosaur spirits are ideal protectors for astral travel due to their distinct qualities:

1. **Primal Strength:** Their raw, untamed energy creates a formidable barrier against harmful entities or disruptive forces.
2. **Resilience:** Dinosaurs thrived in challenging environments, making them adept at maintaining stability in chaotic or unpredictable astral conditions.
3. **Territorial Nature:** Many dinosaur archetypes, like the Tyrannosaurus Rex, are natural protectors, ensuring the safety of those under their care.
4. **Spiritual Guidance:** As ancient beings, they offer wisdom and insight to navigate the astral plane effectively.

Preparing for Astral Travel with Dinosaur Guardians
1. Establish a Connection with Your Dinosaur Guardian
Before enlisting a dinosaur spirit for protection, build a relationship with its energy:

- **Meditate with Dinosaur Archetypes:**
    - Choose a dinosaur archetype that resonates with your intention for astral protection:
        - *Tyrannosaurus Rex*: Fierce defender, strength, and dominance.
        - *Stegosaurus*: Shielding and boundary-setting.
        - *Velociraptor*: Quick reflexes and adaptability in unforeseen situations.
        - *Brontosaurus*: Grounding and stabilizing presence.
        - *Pterodactyl*: Navigational guidance and perspective.
    - Visualize this dinosaur standing beside you, offering its protection and guidance.
- **Create a Sacred Space:**
    - Place fossils, dinosaur figurines, or symbols on your altar to honor and invite their energy.
    - Burn grounding incense such as sandalwood or frankincense to enhance your connection.

2. Set Up Protective Energetic Barriers

- **Crystal Grid for Protection:**
    - Use black tourmaline, obsidian, and clear quartz to create a protective grid around your space.
    - Place a fossil or symbolic item in the center to anchor dinosaur energy.
- **Cleansing Ritual:**
    - Cleanse your body and space with sage, palo santo, or saltwater before beginning astral travel.
    - Envision a glowing sphere of light around you, infused with the energy of your dinosaur guardian.

3. State Your Intention
Clearly articulate your purpose for calling upon a dinosaur spirit. For example:

- "I call upon the spirit of [dinosaur archetype] to stand as my guardian during this journey, protecting me from harm and guiding me through the astral plane."

Techniques for Astral Travel with Dinosaur Guardians
1. Visualization for Astral Protection
This method involves creating a mental image of your dinosaur guardian protecting you as you travel.

1. **Relax and Enter a Meditative State:**
    - Sit or lie down in a comfortable position, focusing on deep, rhythmic breathing.
2. **Summon Your Guardian:**
    - Visualize your chosen dinosaur archetype standing beside you. See its size, shape, and powerful energy radiating strength and protection.
3. **Prepare for Astral Travel:**
    - Imagine your guardian creating a shield around you—a glowing, impenetrable barrier of energy.
4. **Journey into the Astral Plane:**
    - Allow your consciousness to drift into the astral plane, knowing your guardian is by your side.
5. **Return Safely:**
    - When you're ready to return, visualize your guardian guiding you back to your body, ensuring a smooth and secure transition.

2. Guided Invocation Ritual for Astral Protection

This ritual creates a formal connection with a dinosaur spirit to guard your astral journey.

1. **Materials Needed:**
   - A white candle (symbolizing spiritual clarity and safety).
   - A fossil, crystal, or figurine representing your chosen dinosaur.
   - Incense (such as dragon's blood or sage).
2. **Steps:**
   - **Cleanse the Space:**
     - Light the incense and cleanse your ritual area.
   - **Set the Intention:**
     - Hold the fossil or figurine and state your purpose:

Spirit of [dinosaur], guardian of strength and power,
I call upon you in this sacred hour.
Protect my soul as I journey far,
Shield me from harm, my guiding star.

   - **Light the Candle:**
     - Light the candle and visualize its flame connecting you to the dinosaur spirit.
   - **Anchor the Energy:**
     - Place the fossil or figurine near the candle and imagine it glowing with protective energy.
   - **Begin Your Journey:**
     - Close your eyes, relax, and let the guardian's energy envelop you as you enter the astral plane.

3. Pterodactyl's Flight Technique

This technique uses the energy of the Pterodactyl for safe navigation and heightened perspective during astral travel.

1. **Set the Space:**
    - Place a feather or wing-shaped object on your altar to symbolize the Pterodactyl's energy.
2. **Visualize the Pterodactyl:**
    - See it flying above you, scanning the astral landscape for any disturbances or dangers.
3. **Ride the Pterodactyl:**
    - Imagine yourself flying on its back, moving effortlessly through the astral plane. Trust its guidance to lead you to safe and enlightening experiences.
4. **Express Gratitude:**
    - Upon returning, thank the Pterodactyl spirit for its protection and navigation.

Signs of Dinosaur Guardianship During Astral Travel

1. **A Sense of Safety:** You feel a protective presence surrounding you, even in unfamiliar or challenging astral environments.
2. **Visual Cues:** You may see images of your chosen dinosaur or feel its energy guiding and shielding you.
3. **Increased Clarity:** Your journeys are more focused, with clear insights and fewer distractions or disturbances.
4. **Quick Recovery:** Any encounters with unbalanced energies are swiftly resolved, leaving you feeling secure and grounded.

Incorporating Dinosaur Guardians into Daily Practice

1. **Honor Your Guardian:**
    - Create a dedicated space on your altar with items that represent your dinosaur guardian.
    - Leave small offerings, such as herbs, stones, or symbolic tokens, to show appreciation.
2. **Meditate Regularly:**
    - Spend a few minutes each day visualizing your guardian, strengthening your connection and reinforcing their protective role.
3. **Carry a Talisman:**
    - Keep a fossil, crystal, or small figurine with you to maintain a constant link to your guardian's energy.
4. **Dream Work:**
    - Invite your guardian to appear in your dreams, offering protection and guidance as you explore the astral realm in your sleep.

Key Lessons from Dinosaur Guardians

1. **Trust Your Allies:** Dinosaur guardians remind us that even in the vastness of the astral plane, we are never alone.
2. **Strength and Wisdom:** Their energy combines primal power with ancient knowledge, offering both protection and insight.
3. **Balance and Harmony:** Working with these spirits ensures that your astral experiences are enriching, balanced, and aligned with your highest good.
4. **Resilience Through Connection:** By partnering with dinosaur spirits, you develop resilience not just in the astral realm but also in your daily life.

Conclusion

Dinosaur guardians of the astral plane offer a unique and powerful form of protection and guidance, helping you navigate the complexities of psychic exploration with confidence and security. By working with these ancient spirits, you can deepen your astral journeys, uncover profound insights, and return safely to the physical world with renewed wisdom and clarity.

Let the strength of the Tyrannosaurus, the shielding power of the Stegosaurus, and the navigational prowess of the Pterodactyl guide and protect you. With these mighty guardians by your side, the astral plane becomes a realm of empowerment, discovery, and spiritual growth.

Chapter 25: Building a Lifelong Connection with Dinosaur Magick

Dinosaur magick offers a unique blend of primal strength, ancient wisdom, and transformative energy. Developing a lifelong connection with this practice allows you to consistently draw upon its power for guidance, protection, and spiritual growth. Just as dinosaurs were deeply integrated into their ecosystems, you can incorporate their energy into the fabric of your everyday life, creating a dynamic and sustainable spiritual relationship.

In this chapter, we explore strategies for maintaining a consistent connection with dinosaur magick, daily practices to nurture this bond, and ways to deepen your relationship with these ancient energies over time.

Why Build a Lifelong Connection with Dinosaur Magick?

1. **Sustained Growth:** Regular interaction with dinosaur magick helps you grow spiritually, emotionally, and mentally.
2. **Reliable Guidance:** Dinosaur spirits become trusted allies, offering insight and support during life's challenges.
3. **Empowerment and Resilience:** Their energy enhances your ability to navigate change, overcome obstacles, and embrace transformation.
4. **Harmonious Living:** Incorporating their wisdom fosters balance, patience, and alignment with natural cycles.

Core Principles for a Lifelong Practice

To build a lasting relationship with dinosaur magick, focus on these core principles:

1. **Consistency:** Regular practice strengthens your bond with dinosaur spirits and archetypes.
2. **Respect:** Approach dinosaur energy with reverence and gratitude, treating it as a partnership.
3. **Adaptability:** Allow your practice to evolve alongside your spiritual and personal growth.
4. **Integration:** Seamlessly incorporate dinosaur magick into your daily life, making it a natural part of your routines.

Daily Practices to Sustain Your Connection
1. Morning Invocation
Start your day by invoking the energy of a dinosaur archetype aligned with your goals or needs:

- **Example:** Call upon the *Velociraptor* for agility and focus:
    - Light a small candle or hold a talisman.
    - Say:

Spirit of Velociraptor, swift and wise,
Guide me today with sharp focus and clear skies.
Let your energy flow through me,
Bringing success and agility.

2. Evening Reflection
End your day by reflecting on how dinosaur energy supported you and expressing gratitude:

- Journal about moments when you felt their guidance or strength.
- Leave a small offering (e.g., herbs, stones) on your dinosaur altar as a gesture of thanks.

3. Wear or Carry a Dinosaur Talisman

- Keep a fossil, crystal, or dinosaur figurine with you to maintain a constant connection to their energy.
- Choose a talisman that represents the dinosaur archetype you want to align with that day.

4. Meditative Alignment

- Spend 5–10 minutes visualizing your chosen dinosaur archetype.
- Imagine their energy surrounding and supporting you, reinforcing your bond.

Seasonal and Lunar Rituals

Align your dinosaur magick practice with natural cycles to deepen your connection:

1. Seasonal Celebrations

- **Spring:** Work with *Brontosaurus* energy to plant seeds of intention and foster growth.
- **Summer:** Invoke *Tyrannosaurus Rex* for courage and vitality during times of action.
- **Autumn:** Use *Stegosaurus* energy to establish boundaries and prepare for change.
- **Winter:** Embrace *Pterodactyl* for introspection and spiritual perspective.

2. Lunar Phases

- Perform dinosaur magick rituals during specific lunar phases to amplify their energy:
    - **New Moon:** Set intentions with the adaptability of *Velociraptor*.
    - **Full Moon:** Celebrate achievements with the protective energy of *Stegosaurus*.
    - **Waning Moon:** Release negativity with the transformative power of *Tyrannosaurus Rex*.

Maintaining a Dinosaur Altar

A dedicated dinosaur altar serves as a focal point for your magickal practice, providing a space to honor their energy and strengthen your connection.

Elements of a Dinosaur Altar

1. **Representations of Dinosaurs:**
    - Use fossils, figurines, or artwork of your chosen dinosaur archetypes.
2. **Crystals and Stones:**
    - Incorporate petrified wood, ammonite, and other grounding crystals.
3. **Candles and Colors:**
    - Choose colors that correspond to your intentions (e.g., red for strength, green for balance).
4. **Offerings:**
    - Leave herbs, flowers, or symbolic items as tokens of appreciation.
5. **Sacred Tools:**
    - Include tools such as a pendulum, tarot cards, or a journal for divination and reflection.

Deepening Your Connection Over Time
1. Journaling and Reflection

- Keep a dedicated journal to record your experiences with dinosaur magick:
    - Insights from rituals and meditations.
    - Messages or guidance received from dinosaur spirits.
    - Personal growth and milestones achieved with their support.

2. Regular Check-Ins

- Periodically assess your connection with dinosaur magick:
    - Are you consistently incorporating it into your practice?
    - Has your relationship with specific archetypes evolved?
    - What areas of your life can benefit from renewed focus on their energy?

3. Advanced Rituals

As your practice deepens, experiment with more complex rituals, such as:

- Combining multiple dinosaur archetypes for multifaceted intentions.
- Incorporating elemental magick to amplify their energy.

Sharing Dinosaur Magick with Others

One of the most rewarding ways to maintain your connection is by sharing dinosaur magick with your community:

1. Teaching and Guiding

- Offer workshops or write guides to introduce others to dinosaur magick.
- Share your experiences to inspire others to explore this unique spiritual path.

2. Collaborative Rituals

- Gather with like-minded individuals to perform group rituals, calling upon dinosaur spirits for collective goals.

3. Building Community Altars

- Create a shared altar dedicated to dinosaur energy in a public or communal space, allowing others to connect and contribute.

Signs of a Deepened Connection

1. **Synchronicities:** Regularly encountering dinosaur imagery, fossils, or symbols in your daily life.
2. **Enhanced Intuition:** Feeling a stronger connection to your instincts and inner guidance.
3. **Increased Resilience:** Handling challenges with a sense of strength and adaptability inspired by dinosaur energy.
4. **Spiritual Growth:** Experiencing new insights, breakthroughs, or a greater sense of alignment with your purpose.

Potential Challenges and How to Overcome Them
1. Losing Consistency

- **Solution:** Set small, achievable goals for daily practice, such as lighting a candle or holding a talisman.

2. Feeling Disconnected

- **Solution:** Revisit foundational rituals, such as meditating with dinosaur archetypes or cleansing your altar.

3. Overcomplicating the Practice

- **Solution:** Focus on simplicity and authenticity. Even brief moments of connection can be powerful.

Key Lessons from Lifelong Dinosaur Magick

1. **Consistency Builds Strength:** Regular practice ensures a steady and reliable connection to dinosaur energy.
2. **Adaptation is Key:** Just as dinosaurs evolved, allow your practice to change and grow with you.
3. **Power Lies in Balance:** True magick comes from harmonizing strength, wisdom, and patience.
4. **Gratitude Sustains Relationships:** Honor and appreciate dinosaur spirits for their ongoing guidance and protection.

Conclusion

Building a lifelong connection with dinosaur magick is a deeply rewarding journey that enhances every aspect of your spiritual and personal life. By incorporating daily practices, aligning with natural cycles, and nurturing your relationship with dinosaur archetypes, you create a lasting bond with their ancient energy.

As you walk this path, let the wisdom of the dinosaurs guide you, the strength of their spirits empower you, and the resilience of their legacy inspire you. With their energy as a constant presence, you can navigate life's challenges, embrace transformation, and grow into your fullest potential.

Appendices

Appendix A: A Guide to Dinosaur Archetypes and Their Symbolism

This appendix serves as a comprehensive guide to the dinosaur archetypes discussed throughout the book. Each dinosaur embodies unique traits and energies that align with specific aspects of magickal practice and personal growth. The chart below outlines their key traits, symbolic meanings, and suggested magickal uses, providing an easy reference for integrating dinosaur energy into your spiritual journey.

Dinosaur Archetypes and Their Symbolism

Dinosaur	Key Traits	Symbolism	Magickal Uses
Tyrannosaurus Rex	Strength, courage, dominance	Represents raw power, leadership, and the ability to overcome obstacles.	Breaking through barriers, summoning courage, asserting dominance, and amplifying personal power.
Stegosaurus	Protection, resilience, boundaries	Embodies defensive strength and stability, teaching the importance of creating safe boundaries.	Protection spells, establishing emotional or spiritual boundaries, and shielding against negativity.
Brontosaurus	Grounding, patience, endurance	Symbolizes steady growth, perseverance, and connection to the Earth's nurturing energy.	Grounding practices, fostering patience, achieving long-term goals, and creating emotional stability.
Velociraptor	Agility, intellect, adaptability	Reflects quick thinking, strategic action, and the ability to adapt to changing circumstances.	Enhancing mental clarity, overcoming challenges, increasing flexibility, and achieving swift progress.

Dinosaur	Key Traits	Symbolism	Magickal Uses
Pterodactyl	Freedom, perspective, spiritual ascension	Represents liberation, higher vision, and the ability to rise above obstacles for clarity.	Astral travel, dreamwork, gaining insight, and achieving spiritual growth through higher perspectives.
Triceratops	Defense, assertiveness, voice	Stands for self-expression, assertive action, and the power to protect oneself and others.	Strengthening communication, standing up for oneself, and creating a shield of emotional or physical defense.
Ankylosaurus	Fortification, stability, persistence	Represents unshakable strength and the ability to withstand challenges without losing integrity.	Building resilience, reinforcing spiritual armor, and creating strong foundations in magickal practices.
Brachiosaurus	Wisdom, balance, long-term success	Embodies harmony, thoughtful action, and the pursuit of higher understanding.	Balancing power with wisdom, achieving harmony, and aligning actions with long-term spiritual growth.
Spinosaurus	Fluidity, adaptability, dominance	Combines strength with versatility, particularly in challenging or transitional environments.	Embracing change, navigating emotional or spiritual waters, and asserting power in unfamiliar situations.
Pachycephalosaurus	Focus, determination, mental strength	Symbolizes persistence and intellectual fortitude, with a focus on overcoming mental obstacles.	Strengthening mental clarity, enhancing concentration, and breaking through mental barriers.

Dinosaur Archetype Details

Tyrannosaurus Rex

- **Key Traits:** Strength, leadership, boldness.
- **Symbolism:** The ultimate warrior, the T. rex teaches us to face challenges head-on and assert our power without hesitation.
- **Magickal Uses:** Courage rituals, empowerment spells, and overcoming fear.
- **Associated Crystals:** Carnelian, tiger's eye.
- **Elemental Connection:** Fire.

Stegosaurus

- **Key Traits:** Protection, resilience, stability.
- **Symbolism:** A guardian of boundaries, the Stegosaurus reminds us to shield ourselves from negativity while standing firm.
- **Magickal Uses:** Protection wards, grounding rituals, and emotional fortification.
- **Associated Crystals:** Black tourmaline, obsidian.
- **Elemental Connection:** Earth.

Brontosaurus

- **Key Traits:** Grounding, patience, longevity.
- **Symbolism:** The Brontosaurus embodies steady growth and rooted energy, helping us remain grounded during challenging times.
- **Magickal Uses:** Grounding meditations, stability spells, and long-term goal setting.
- **Associated Crystals:** Petrified wood, smoky quartz.
- **Elemental Connection:** Earth.

Velociraptor

- **Key Traits:** Agility, adaptability, strategy.
- **Symbolism:** This swift and clever dinosaur teaches us to think on our feet and adapt to ever-changing situations.
- **Magickal Uses:** Quick decision-making, enhancing mental clarity, and overcoming obstacles.
- **Associated Crystals:** Clear quartz, citrine.
- **Elemental Connection:** Air.

Pterodactyl

- Key Traits: Freedom, perspective, spiritual elevation.
- Symbolism: The Pterodactyl's ability to soar high symbolizes liberation from constraints and clarity of vision.
- Magickal Uses: Astral projection, gaining insight, and connecting with higher realms.
- Associated Crystals: Selenite, clear quartz.
- Elemental Connection: Air.

Triceratops

- Key Traits: Assertiveness, protection, communication.
- Symbolism: With its iconic horns, the Triceratops symbolizes the courage to stand up for oneself and communicate with authority.
- Magickal Uses: Enhancing self-expression, creating energetic shields, and standing firm in confrontations.
- Associated Crystals: Amazonite, aquamarine.
- Elemental Connection: Earth.

Ankylosaurus

- Key Traits: Fortification, persistence, stability.
- Symbolism: This armored dinosaur teaches us to build strong defenses and stand unyielding against challenges.
- Magickal Uses: Building resilience, reinforcing boundaries, and strengthening spiritual protection.
- Associated Crystals: Hematite, onyx.
- Elemental Connection: Earth.

Brachiosaurus

- Key Traits: Balance, wisdom, growth.
- Symbolism: With its towering height and serene demeanor, the Brachiosaurus embodies harmony and higher understanding.
- Magickal Uses: Balancing power with wisdom, achieving long-term success, and cultivating patience.
- Associated Crystals: Amethyst, moss agate.
- Elemental Connection: Earth and Air.

Spinosaurus

- **Key Traits:** Fluidity, versatility, adaptability.
- **Symbolism:** This semi-aquatic dinosaur represents the balance between power and flexibility, teaching us to thrive in uncertain environments.
- **Magickal Uses:** Navigating transitions, embracing change, and aligning with emotional fluidity.
- **Associated Crystals:** Aquamarine, moonstone.
- **Elemental Connection:** Water.

Pachycephalosaurus

- **Key Traits:** Focus, mental strength, determination.
- **Symbolism:** Known for its thick skull, this dinosaur teaches us to push through mental blocks and stay committed to our goals.
- **Magickal Uses:** Enhancing concentration, overcoming intellectual challenges, and strengthening focus.
- **Associated Crystals:** Fluorite, sodalite.
- **Elemental Connection:** Air.

Using This Guide

To incorporate dinosaur archetypes into your magickal practice:

1. **Choose the Archetype:** Select the dinosaur whose traits align with your intention.
2. **Work with the Symbolism:** Meditate on the archetype's lessons and how they relate to your life.
3. **Use Correspondences:** Incorporate the associated crystals, colors, and elements into your rituals.
4. **Build Relationships:** Spend time connecting with your chosen dinosaur archetype to deepen your understanding and strengthen your practice.

Conclusion

This guide to dinosaur archetypes provides a foundation for understanding the symbolic and magickal potential of these ancient beings. By aligning with their unique energies, you can tap into a diverse range of strengths and wisdom to empower your spiritual journey and enrich your life. Let this chart be your companion as you explore the boundless possibilities of dinosaur magick.

Appendix B: Fossil Hunting for Magickal Practitioners

Fossils and bones are powerful tools for magickal practitioners, serving as tangible links to the ancient past and the energies of prehistoric Earth. Incorporating fossils into your practice can enhance grounding, amplify intention, and strengthen your connection to dinosaur spirits and archetypes. However, sourcing these materials ethically and using them with respect and purpose is crucial to preserving their integrity and honoring their origins.

This appendix provides tips for finding, purchasing, and using fossils and bones in a magickal context while maintaining ethical and sustainable practices.

Understanding the Magickal Significance of Fossils

Fossils hold unique energy and symbolism that makes them invaluable in magickal work:

1. **Ancient Energy:** Fossils carry the essence of millions of years, connecting you to Earth's cycles and wisdom.
2. **Grounding Power:** Their deep connection to the Earth provides stability and grounding during rituals and meditations.
3. **Transformation:** Fossils symbolize the process of change and evolution, making them ideal for transformational magick.
4. **Link to Dinosaur Spirits:** Fossils act as physical anchors for connecting with the spirits of dinosaurs and other ancient beings.

Ethical Fossil Sourcing
1. Understand Legal and Ethical Guidelines

- **Know the Laws:** Research fossil collection laws in your area or the area where you plan to source fossils. Many regions have strict regulations to protect historical and scientific artifacts.
    - For example, in the U.S., collecting fossils from public lands often requires a permit, and collecting on private property requires the landowner's permission.
- **Avoid Protected Sites:** Never collect fossils from national parks, heritage sites, or other protected areas.

2. Purchase from Reputable Dealers

- Seek out ethical fossil dealers who source their materials responsibly and adhere to legal guidelines.
    - Look for dealers with clear provenance records (the history of the fossil's discovery and ownership).
    - Avoid dealers who sell fossils obtained from looting or illegal excavations.
- Support fossil shops associated with museums or scientific institutions, as these often have strict ethical standards.

3. Practice Responsible Collecting
If you choose to collect fossils yourself:

- **Research Locations:** Identify areas where fossil collection is allowed and encouraged.
- **Use Proper Tools:** Carry small brushes, hammers, and chisels designed for fossil hunting to minimize damage.
- **Leave Significant Finds:** If you uncover a rare or scientifically significant fossil, report it to local authorities or museums instead of keeping it.
- **Respect the Environment:** Avoid disrupting ecosystems or removing excessive material from the site.

4. Avoid Exploitation

- Be wary of purchasing fossils that may have been sourced from vulnerable communities or sold under exploitative conditions.
- Choose alternatives, such as replicas or local, non-endangered fossils, if ethical concerns arise.

Cleansing and Preparing Fossils for Magickal Use

Before using fossils in your practice, cleanse and prepare them to remove lingering energy and attune them to your intentions.

1. Physical Cleaning

- Use a soft brush to remove dirt or debris from the fossil.
- For delicate specimens, gently rinse them with water and allow them to air dry.

2. Energetic Cleansing

- **Smoke Cleansing:** Pass the fossil through the smoke of sage, palo santo, or another cleansing herb to remove residual energy.
- **Salt Cleansing:** Place the fossil in a bowl of salt for 24 hours to absorb unwanted energy. Avoid this method for delicate or porous fossils.
- **Moonlight Cleansing:** Leave the fossil under the light of the full moon to purify and charge it with lunar energy.

3. Intentional Programming

- Hold the fossil in your hands and visualize it glowing with energy. State your intention clearly, such as:

This fossil, a relic of the ancient Earth,
Holds the wisdom of eons past.
I dedicate it to my practice,
For grounding, transformation, and connection.

Using Fossils in Magickal Practices

Fossils can be integrated into your magickal work in a variety of ways:

1. Grounding and Stabilizing

- Hold a fossil during meditation to anchor your energy and enhance your connection to the Earth.
- Place fossils on your altar or in your sacred space to create a grounding energy field.

2. Channeling Ancient Wisdom

- Use fossils as a focus for connecting with the spirits of dinosaurs or other ancient beings.
- Meditate with the fossil to receive insights or messages from the past.

3. Enhancing Spells and Rituals

- Incorporate fossils into spells for transformation, protection, or resilience.
- Place a fossil on your ritual tools (e.g., candles, wands) to amplify their energy.

4. Divination

- Use fossils as a tool for scrying or as part of a divination set, alongside crystals or runes.
- Ask the fossil for guidance on specific questions, allowing its energy to inform your intuition.

5. Crafting Talismans

- Wear fossils as jewelry or carry them as talismans to maintain a constant connection to their energy.
- Combine fossils with other materials (e.g., crystals, herbs) to create custom charms.

Fossil Care and Maintenance

To maintain the integrity and energy of your fossils:

1. **Handle with Care:**
    - Avoid dropping or scratching delicate fossils.
    - Store them in a safe, dry place away from direct sunlight or extreme temperatures.
2. **Refresh Energetic Cleansing:**
    - Periodically cleanse and recharge your fossils, especially after intense rituals or emotional work.
3. **Rotate Usage:**
    - Alternate the fossils you use to prevent overuse and maintain their energetic balance.
4. **Honor Their Legacy:**
    - Treat fossils with respect, recognizing their role as ancient relics and powerful spiritual tools.

Alternatives to Fossils

If sourcing fossils is difficult or if ethical concerns arise, consider these alternatives:

1. **Replica Fossils:** High-quality replicas can be charged with intention and used effectively in magickal work.
2. **Petrified Wood:** This easily accessible material holds grounding and transformative energy similar to fossils.
3. **Crystals with Fossil Energy:** Stones like ammonite, orthoceras, or fossilized coral carry the essence of ancient life.

Fossil Types and Their Magickal Correspondences

Fossil Type	Symbolism	Magickal Uses
Ammonite	Cycles, transformation, protection	Use for grounding, shielding, and connecting to the cycles of life.
Fossilized Coral	Emotional stability, resilience	Incorporate into rituals for emotional healing and balance.
Trilobite	Adaptability, survival, evolution	Use for overcoming challenges and embracing personal growth.
Petrified Wood	Strength, grounding, endurance	Ideal for grounding practices, patience spells, and connecting with Earth's ancient energy.
Dinosaur Bone Fragments	Power, strength, ancestral energy	Use to channel dinosaur spirits, summon courage, and build resilience.

Conclusion

Fossils offer an extraordinary connection to Earth's ancient past, serving as powerful tools for grounding, transformation, and spiritual growth. By sourcing fossils ethically, cleansing and preparing them, and incorporating them mindfully into your practice, you can harness their immense energy and wisdom while honoring their origins.

Treat fossils with respect and reverence, recognizing their role as both scientific treasures and spiritual allies. With care and intention, fossils can become invaluable companions on your magickal journey, linking you to the timeless cycles of the Earth and the enduring strength of its ancient inhabitants.

Appendix C: Dinosaur Magick Correspondences

In magickal practices, correspondences—associations between spiritual energies and tangible elements—serve as powerful tools for amplifying intention and focusing energy. For dinosaur magick, these correspondences deepen your connection to specific dinosaur archetypes and enhance the effectiveness of your rituals and spells.

This appendix provides a comprehensive list of correspondences for each dinosaur archetype, including colors, crystals, herbs, planetary influences, elements, and suggested tools. These associations are tailored to reflect the unique traits and symbolism of each dinosaur.

Dinosaur Magick Correspondences

1. Tyrannosaurus Rex

- **Traits:** Strength, courage, dominance.
- **Colors:** Red, gold, crimson.
- **Crystals:** Carnelian, tiger's eye, red jasper.
- **Herbs:** Ginger, cayenne, dragon's blood.
- **Planetary Influences:** Mars (strength and aggression), Sun (power and vitality).
- **Element:** Fire.
- **Suggested Tools:** Claw-shaped objects, sharp stones, weapons (symbolic or ritualized).
- **Magickal Uses:** Empowerment, overcoming fear, breaking through obstacles, leadership.

2. Stegosaurus

- **Traits:** Protection, resilience, boundaries.
- **Colors:** Green, black, earthy tones.
- **Crystals:** Black tourmaline, obsidian, hematite.
- **Herbs:** Sage, rosemary, yarrow.
- **Planetary Influences:** Saturn (protection and structure), Earth (grounding and stability).
- **Element:** Earth.
- **Suggested Tools:** Shields (symbolic or physical), spiked or plate-like stones.
- **Magickal Uses:** Defensive magick, boundary setting, protection wards, stability.

3. Brontosaurus

- **Traits:** Grounding, patience, long-term success.
- **Colors:** Brown, moss green, deep gray.
- **Crystals:** Petrified wood, smoky quartz, moss agate.
- **Herbs:** Oak, myrrh, valerian root.
- **Planetary Influences:** Earth (steadiness and growth), Venus (harmony and nurturing).
- **Element:** Earth.
- **Suggested Tools:** Fossils, wooden tools, Earth-colored candles.

- **Magickal Uses:** Grounding rituals, perseverance, fostering patience, long-term goal manifestation.

4. Velociraptor

- **Traits:** Agility, intellect, adaptability.
- **Colors:** Yellow, orange, silver.
- **Crystals:** Citrine, fluorite, clear quartz.
- **Herbs:** Lemongrass, cinnamon, thyme.
- **Planetary Influences:** Mercury (quick thinking and adaptability), Air (clarity and communication).
- **Element:** Air.
- **Suggested Tools:** Feathers, sleek stones, tools for swift motion (e.g., pendulums).
- **Magickal Uses:** Enhancing mental clarity, adaptability spells, quick decision-making.

5. Pterodactyl

- **Traits:** Freedom, perspective, spiritual ascension.
- **Colors:** White, silver, sky blue.
- **Crystals:** Selenite, moonstone, angelite.
- **Herbs:** Lavender, eucalyptus, white sage.
- **Planetary Influences:** Uranus (freedom and innovation), Air (clarity and higher thought).
- **Element:** Air.
- **Suggested Tools:** Feathers, wing-shaped objects, incense.
- **Magickal Uses:** Astral travel, dreamwork, gaining insight, spiritual elevation.

6. Triceratops

- **Traits:** Assertiveness, defense, voice.
- **Colors:** Dark green, turquoise, steel gray.
- **Crystals:** Amazonite, aquamarine, turquoise.
- **Herbs:** Basil, mint, fennel.
- **Planetary Influences:** Mars (assertiveness), Mercury (communication).
- **Element:** Earth.
- **Suggested Tools:** Horn-shaped objects, blue candles.
- **Magickal Uses:** Strengthening communication, emotional defense, asserting personal power.

7. Ankylosaurus

- **Traits:** Fortification, stability, persistence.
- **Colors:** Black, deep brown, forest green.
- **Crystals:** Onyx, hematite, garnet.
- **Herbs:** Patchouli, mugwort, cedar.
- **Planetary Influences:** Saturn (stability and protection), Earth (grounding).
- **Element:** Earth.
- **Suggested Tools:** Heavy stones, armor-like materials, solid objects.
- **Magickal Uses:** Creating spiritual armor, resilience spells, fortifying boundaries.

8. Brachiosaurus

- **Traits:** Wisdom, balance, long-term growth.
- **Colors:** Violet, deep blue, soft gray.
- **Crystals:** Amethyst, sodalite, lapis lazuli.
- **Herbs:** Lavender, chamomile, willow bark.
- **Planetary Influences:** Jupiter (wisdom and growth), Venus (balance and harmony).
- **Element:** Earth and Air.
- **Suggested Tools:** Tall candles, fossils, symbolic trees or branches.
- **Magickal Uses:** Balancing power and wisdom, achieving harmony, spiritual alignment.

9. Spinosaurus

- **Traits:** Fluidity, versatility, dominance.
- **Colors:** Teal, aquamarine, deep blue.
- **Crystals:** Aquamarine, moonstone, labradorite.
- **Herbs:** Water mint, lotus, seaweed.
- **Planetary Influences:** Neptune (intuition and fluidity), Water (emotions and adaptability).
- **Element:** Water.
- **Suggested Tools:** Water bowls, reflective surfaces, spiral-shaped objects.
- **Magickal Uses:** Navigating transitions, emotional healing, fluidity in decision-making.

10. Pachycephalosaurus

- **Traits:** Focus, determination, mental strength.
- **Colors:** Indigo, navy blue, silver.
- **Crystals:** Fluorite, sodalite, lapis lazuli.
- **Herbs:** Peppermint, rosemary, sage.
- **Planetary Influences:** Mercury (focus and intellect), Air (mental clarity).
- **Element:** Air.

- **Suggested Tools:** Smooth, rounded stones, head-shaped symbols.
- **Magickal Uses:** Enhancing concentration, mental resilience, overcoming obstacles.

Using Correspondences in Dinosaur Magick

1. **Color Magick:**
    - Incorporate the colors associated with your chosen dinosaur into candles, altar cloths, or clothing during rituals.
2. **Crystal Work:**
    - Use the crystals linked to a specific dinosaur to amplify their energy. Place them on your altar, carry them as talismans, or hold them during meditation.
3. **Herbal Enhancements:**
    - Burn the corresponding herbs as incense, create herbal sachets, or incorporate them into potions to align with the dinosaur's energy.
4. **Planetary Timing:**
    - Align your rituals with the planetary influences of the dinosaur for maximum effectiveness. For example, work with *Tyrannosaurus Rex* energy on a Tuesday (Mars' day) to amplify courage.
5. **Symbolic Tools:**
    - Integrate the suggested tools—such as fossils, feathers, or stones—into your magickal practice to focus and direct the dinosaur's energy.

Conclusion

These correspondences serve as a foundational guide for incorporating dinosaur archetypes into your magickal practices. By aligning your tools, timing, and intentions with the unique energies of these ancient beings, you can create more focused, powerful, and transformative rituals. Let this appendix be your resource for crafting spells, meditations, and rituals that honor the timeless strength and wisdom of the dinosaurs.

Message from the Author:

I hope you enjoyed this book, I love astrology and knew there was not a book such as this out on the shelf. I love metaphysical items as well. Please check out my other books:

-Life of Government Benefits
-My life of Hell
-My life with Hydrocephalus
-Red Sky
-World Domination:Woman's rule
-World Domination:Woman's Rule 2: The War
-Life and Banishment of Apophis: book 1
-The Kidney Friendly Diet
-The Ultimate Hemp Cookbook
-Creating a Dispensary(legally)
-Cleanliness throughout life: the importance of showering from childhood to adulthood.
-Strong Roots: The Risks of Overcoddling children
-Hemp Horoscopes: Cosmic Insights and Earthly Healing
- Celestial Hemp Navigating the Zodiac: Through the Green Cosmos
-Astrological Hemp: Aligning The Stars with Earth's Ancient Herb
-The Astrological Guide to Hemp: Stars, Signs, and Sacred Leaves
-Green Growth: Innovative Marketing Strategies for your Hemp Products and Dispensary
-Cosmic Cannabis
-Astrological Munchies
-Henry The Hemp
-Zodiacal Roots: The Astrological Soul Of Hemp
- **Green Constellations: Intersection of Hemp and Zodiac**
-Hemp in The Houses: An astrological Adventure Through The Cannabis Galaxy
-Galactic Ganja Guide
Heavenly Hemp
Zodiac Leaves
Doctor Who Astrology
Cannastrology
Stellar Satvias and Cosmic Indicas

<u>Celestial Cannabis: A Zodiac Journey</u>
AstroHerbology: The Sky and The Soil: Volume 1
AstroHerbology:Celestial Cannabis:Volume 2
Cosmic Cannabis Cultivation
The Starry Guide to Herbal Harmony: Volume 1
The Starry Guide to Herbal Harmony: Cannabis Universe: Volume 2
Yugioh Astrology: Astrological Guide to Deck, Duels and more
Nightmare Mansion: Echoes of The Abyss
Nightmare Mansion 2: Legacy of Shadows
Nightmare Mansion 3: Shadows of the Forgotten
Nightmare Mansion 4: Echoes of the Damned
The Life and Banishment of Apophis: Book 2
Nightmare Mansion: Halls of Despair
<u>Healing with Herb: Cannabis and Hydrocephalus</u>
<u>Planetary Pot: Aligning with Astrological Herbs: Volume 1</u>
Fast Track to Freedom: 30 Days to Financial Independence Using AI, Assets, and Agile Hustles
<u>Cosmic Hemp Pathways</u>
How to Become Financially Free in 30 Days: 10,000 Paths to Prosperity
Zodiacal Herbage: Astrological Insights: Volume 1
Nightmare Mansion: Whispers in the Walls
The Daleks Invade Atlantis
Henry the hemp and Hydrocephalus

10X The Kidney Friendly Diet
Cannabis Universe: Adult coloring book
Hemp Astrology: The Healing Power of the Stars
Zodiacal Herbage: Astrological Insights: Cannabis Universe: Volume 2
<u>Planetary Pot: Aligning with Astrological Herbs: Cannabis Universes: Volume 2</u>
Doctor Who Meets the Replicators and SG-1: The Ultimate Battle for Survival
Nightmare Mansion: Curse of the Blood Moon
<u>The Celestial Stoner: A Guide to the Zodiac</u>
Cosmic Pleasures: Sex Toy Astrology for Every Sign
Hydrocephalus Astrology: Navigating the Stars and Healing Waters
Lapis and the Mischievous Chocolate Bar

Celestial Positions: Sexual Astrology for Every Sign
Apophis's Shadow Work Journal: : A Journey of Self-Discovery and Healing
Kinky Cosmos: Sexual Kink Astrology for Every Sign
Digital Cosmos: The Astrological Digimon Compendium
Stellar Seeds: The Cosmic Guide to Growing with Astrology

Apophis's Daily Gratitude Journal

Cat Astrology: Feline Mysteries of the Cosmos
The Cosmic Kama Sutra: An Astrological Guide to Sexual Positions
Unleash Your Potential: A Guided Journal Powered by AI Insights
Whispers of the Enchanted Grove

Cosmic Pleasures: An Astrological Guide to Sexual Kinks
369, 12 Manifestation Journal
Whisper of the nocturne journal(blank journal for writing or drawing)
The Boogey Book
Locked In Reflection: A Chastity Journey Through Locktober
Generating Wealth Quickly:
How to Generate $100,000 in 24 Hours
Star Magic: Harness the Power of the Universe
The Flatulence Chronicles: A Fart Journal for Self-Discovery
The Doctor and The Death Moth
Seize the Day: A Personal Seizure Tracking Journal
The Ultimate Boogeyman Safari: A Journey into the Boogie World and Beyond
Whispers of Samhain: 1,000 Spells of Love, Luck, and Lunar Magic: Samhain Spell Book
Apophis's guides:
Witch's Spellbook Crafting Guide for Halloween
<u>**Frost & Flame: The Enchanted Yule Grimoire of 1000 Winter Spells**</u>
<u>**The Ultimate Boogey Goo Guide & Spooky Activities for Halloween Fun**</u>
Harmony of the Scales: A Libra's Spellcraft for Balance and Beauty
The Enchanted Advent: 36 Days of Christmas Wonders

Nightmare Mansion: The Labyrinth of Screams
Harvest of Enchantment: 1,000 Spells of Gratitude, Love, and Fortune for Thanksgiving
The Boogey Chronicles: A Journal of Nightly Encounters and Shadowy Secrets
The 12 Days of Financial Freedom: A Step-by-Step Christmas Countdown to Transform Your Finances
Sigil of the Eternal Spiral Blank Journal
A Christmas Feast: Timeless Recipes for Every Meal
Holiday Stress-Free Solutions: A Survival Guide to Thriving During the Festive Season
Yu-Gi-Oh! Holiday Gifting Mastery: The Ultimate Guide for Fans and Newcomers Alike
Holiday Harmony: A Hydrocephalus Survival Guide for the Festive Season
Celestial Craft: The Witch's Almanac for 2025 – A Cosmic Guide to Manifestations, Moons, and Mystical Events
Doctor Who: The Toymaker's Winter Wonderland
Tulsa King Unveiled: A Thrilling Guide to Stallone's Mafia Masterpiece

Pendulum Craft: A Complete Guide to Crafting and Using Personalized Divination Tools
Nightmare Mansion: Santa's Eternal Eve
Starlight Noel: A Cosmic Journey through Christmas Mysteries
The Dark Architect: Unlocking the Blueprint of Existence
Surviving the Embrace: The Ultimate Guide to Encounters with The Hugging Molly
The Enchanted Codex: Secrets of the Craft for Witches, Wiccans, and Pagans
Harvest of Gratitude: A Complete Thanksgiving Guide
Yuletide Essentials: A Complete Guide to an Authentic and Magical Christmas
Celestial Smokes: A Cosmic Guide to Cigars and Astrology
Living in Balance: A Comprehensive Survival Guide to Thriving with Diabetes Insipidus
Cosmic Symbiosis: The Venom Zodiac Chronicles
The Cursed Paw of Ambition
Cosmic Symbiosis: The Astrological Venom Journal
Celestial Wonders Unfold: A Stargazer's Guide to the Cosmos (2024-2029)
The Ultimate Black Friday Prepper's Guide: Mastering Shopping Strategies and Savings
Cosmic Sales: The Astrological Guide to Black Friday Shopping
Legends of the Corn Mother and Other Harvest Myths
Whispers of the Harvest: The Corn Mother's Journal
The Evergreen Spellbook
The Doctor Meets the Boogeyman
The White Witch of Rose Hall's SpellBook
The Gingerbread Golem's Shadow: A Study in Sweet Darkness
The Gingerbread Golem Codex: An Academic Exploration of Sweet Myths
The Gingerbread Golem Grimoire: Sweet Magicks and Spells for the Festive Witch
The Curse of the Gingerbread Golem
10-minute Christmas Crafts for kids
<u>Christmas Crisis Solutions: The Ultimate Last-Minute Survival Guide</u>
Gingerbread Golem Recipes: Holiday Treats with a Magical Twist
The Infinite Key: Unlocking Mystical Secrets of the Ages
Enchanted Yule: A Wiccan and Pagan Guide to a Magical and Memorable Season

If you want solar for your home go here: https://www.harborsolar.live/apophisenterprises/

Get Some Tarot cards: https://www.makeplayingcards.com/sell/apophis-occult-shop

Get some shirts: https://www.bonfire.com/store/apophis-shirt-emporium/

Instagrams:
@apophis_enterprises,
@apophisbookemporium,
@apophisscardshop
Twitter: @apophisenterpr1
Tiktok:@apophisenterprise
Youtube: @sg1fan23477, @FiresideRetreatKingdom
Hive: @sg1fan23477
CheeLee: @SG1fan23477

Podcast: Apophis Chat Zone: https://open.spotify.com/show/5zXbr-CLEV2xzCp8ybrfHsk?si=fb4d4fdbdce44dec

Newsletter: https://apophiss-newsletter-27c897.beehiiv.com/

Milton Keynes UK
Ingram Content Group UK Ltd.
UKHW052014111224
452349UK00012B/150

9 798330 631513